IGLOO

CONTEMPORARY VERNACULAR ARCHITECTURE

ALEJANDRO BAHAMÓN
ANA CAÑIZARES

I0803817

Schiffer Publishing Ltd
4880 Lower Valley Road • Atglen, PA 19310

Managing editor: María Fernanda Canal

Editors: Alejandro Bahamón and Ana Cañizares

Text for first section: Àgata Losantos

Text on projects: Maria Rosa Badia Gener

Research: Alexandre Campello

Art direction: Mídori

Graphic design: Montse Montero / Soti Mas-Bagà

Project management:
latinta
www.latinta.net

Originally published as *Iglú de Arquitectura Vernácula a Contemporánea* by Parramón Press, Inc.

Translated from Spanish by Omicron Language Solutions, LLC

Copyright ©2012 by Schiffer Publishing, Ltd.
Library of Congress Control Number: 2012948274

All rights reserved. No part of this work may be reproduced or used in any form or by any means—graphic, electronic, or mechanical, including photocopying or information storage and retrieval systems—without written permission from the publisher.
The scanning, uploading and distribution of this book or any part thereof via the Internet or via any other means without the permission of the publisher is illegal and punishable by law. Please purchase only authorized editions and do not participate in or encourage the electronic piracy of copyrighted materials.
"Schiffer," "Schiffer Publishing, Ltd. & Design," and the "Design of pen and inkwell" are registered trademarks of Schiffer Publishing, Ltd.

Cover Adaptation by RoS
Design Adaptation by Stephanie Daugherty
Type set in Formata Regular/DIN-Regular
ISBN: 978-0-7643-4192-2
Printed in China

Other Schiffer Books on Related Subjects:
Mexican Style, Sustainable,
978-0-7643-2743-8, $19.95
Green Homes: Dwellings for the 21st Century,
978-0-7643-3033-9, $39.99
Wood in Traditional Architecture,
978-0-7643-3581-5, $45.00
Stone in Traditional Architecture,
978-0-7643-3614-0, $45.00

Published by
SCHIFFER PUBLISHING, LTD
4880 Lower Valley Road
Atglen, PA 19310
Phone: (610) 593-1777
Fax: (610) 593-2002
E-mail: Info@schifferbooks.com
Website: www.schifferbooks.com

For the largest selection of fine reference books on this and related subjects, please visit our website. You may also write for a free catalog.
This book may be purchased from the publisher. Please try your bookstore first.
We are always looking for people to write books on new and related subjects. If you have an idea for a book, please contact us at proposals@schifferbooks.com

Schiffer Books are available at special discounts for bulk purchases for sales promotions or premiums. Special editions, including personalized covers, corporate imprints, and excerpts can be created in large quantities for special needs. For more information contact the publisher.

In Europe, Schiffer books are distributed by
BUSHWOOD BOOKS
6 Marksbury Ave.
Kew Gardens
Surrey TW9 4JF England
Phone: 44 (0) 20 8392 8585;
Fax: 44 (0) 20 8392 9876
E-mail: info@bushwoodbooks.co.uk
Website: www.bushwoodbooks.co.uk

INTRODUCTION

Alejandro Bahamón

Of the vast variety of types of vernacular architecture, the igloo is probably the one which provokes the most curiosity and affection. The contrast between the frozen exterior landscape and the home created inside it, the efficiency of its structure linked to a building system, or the peculiarity of being made with a material that vanishes without a trace are some of the characteristics which have given rise to its fascination and have been analyzed for centuries. This particular dwelling, developed by the Inuit cultures in the Arctic region, is a direct response to the nomadic style of living, the extreme climatic conditions, and the scarcity of resources. Like other vernacular structures, it is an architectural form which facilitates a basic function of human existence in the most effective way possible, and constitutes a significant trait of the cultural identity of its people. A clear understanding of the characteristic traits that define the igloo, the process of its construction, and its relationship with the environment are of great importance in architecture and contemporary design. This book, in addition to putting forward a detailed analysis of the traditional way of thinking about igloos, gathers together the work of architects, designers, and artists from around the world who have turned their attention to this unique compacted dome of snow when planning some of their work, or, given the unique traits of the project as well as the igloo, have given us an interesting relationship to explore. An important compilation that shows the connections between vernacular and contemporary design, it establishes a valuable channel of architectural research and represents a celebration of a form of building thousands of years old which, due to globalization and global warming, is seeing its very existence threatened for the first time.

VERNACULAR ARCHITECTURE AND THE IGLOO

■ GEOGRAPHICAL AREAS WHERE THE VERNACULAR IGLOO CAN BE FOUND

VERNACULAR ARCHITECTURE AND THE IGLOO

When we think about the great milestones of architecture, it is unlikely that it occurs to us to include ephemeral anonymous works built in regions as remote as the Arctic. This *other* architecture, grouped together as vernacular, did not begin to attract the interest of the official face of architecture, leaving aside older focuses of a folkloric nature, until the main advantages of their construction came to light again in the twentieth century. As diverse as the cultural communities and habitats in the world, vernacular architecture shares a number a qualities to which the most recent architect-designed architecture aspires: efficiency, good sense, honesty, and economy. Despite its invisibility, a consequence of its usual remote location and its rare presence in the media, vernacular architecture makes up 90% of existing structures, far from fashion trends or the latest technological advances.

Tatigat, an Inuk, slides a snow block over the door of his igloo at dusk. Igloolik, Nunavut, Canada.

Of the many examples of vernacular architecture, all linked to an actual culture, environment, and climate, there is one of great iconic power that, due to its precarious existence, deserves to have the leading role in this compilation. The protagonist of this book is the igloo, traditional refuge of the semi-nomadic Inuit people, or as they are more popularly known, the Eskimo people. The Inuit lived for thousands of years isolated from the rest of the world in the inhospitable region situated north of the Arctic Circle, a condition which reinforced their cultural behavior and strong sense of group identity. This peculiarity, together with their surrounding habitat, strongly determined the simple sophistication of their winter dwelling.

In one land, in the difficult Arctic region, survival was only guaranteed by the ability to erect a refuge quickly to keep out of the freezing temperatures and offer protection from the elements with nothing more than snow. This refuge is the igloo, considered by some to be the most splendid, ingenious, and varied of the nomadic structures.

On the other hand, as the traditional dwelling of the Inuit, the igloo is the backdrop, where, since ancestral times, they have lived and worshipped, repeating and reinforcing the beliefs which shape this Arctic culture. As we will see later, it is from here that the symbolic value of this structure comes, whose shape, which mirrors in detail the rituals which go on inside it, reflects the social structure of the Inuit (the hierarchies of the group, as well as the individual tasks attributed to each member), and its cosmology (the division between sea and earth or the male and female worlds).

Therefore, given the fundamental role of the igloo as holder and preserver of the Inuit culture, the progressive loss of the sense of tradition and the new ways of life brought on by the overwhelming advance of globalization put their continuation in serious danger. In addition, the igloo also has to deal with one more threat than those posed to other traditional vernacular structures: global warming, whose effects are especially notable and accelerated in the Poles. According to the Inuit, the

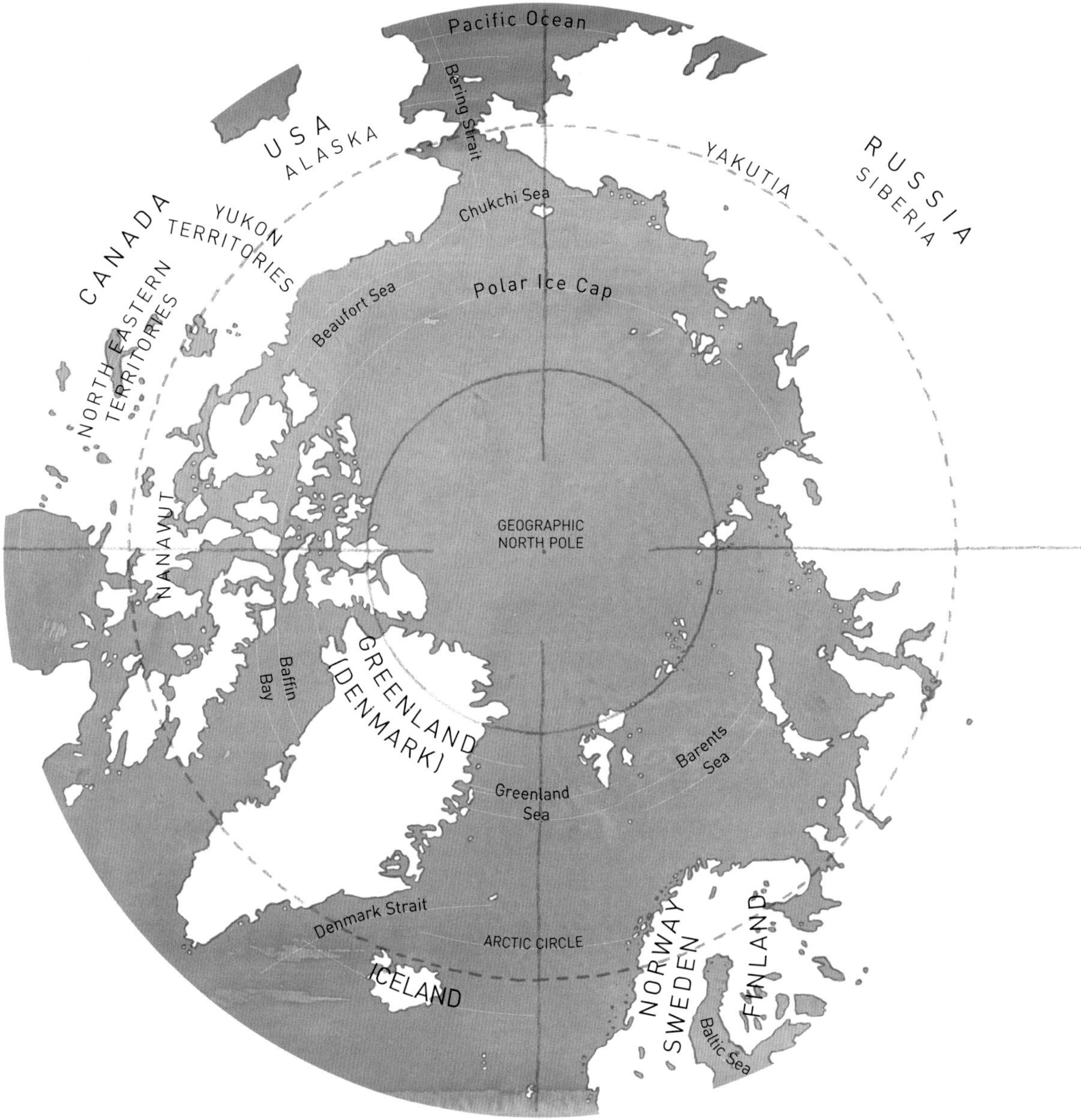

Map of the Polar Arctic where the Inuit population are dispersed

quality of the snow is worsening, which makes the construction of long lasting igloos difficult. In addition to this, due to the change in the prevailing winds, the landscape is transforming rapidly and the old orientation landmarks are being eliminated. Despite all these difficulties, the Inuit, born survivors, are adapting to the new world that has been imposed on them in the last few decades. The igloo, on the other hand has less promising prospects. With the increasing scarcity of building materials and the lifestyle that brought it about dying out, this brilliant archi-

tectural solution is heading towards a progressive disappearance that can only be stopped if the essence of the igloo is recovered and reinterpreted in contemporary architecture. It is precisely this desire to keep the igloo alive, not to mention the environment and culture to which it belongs—an instinct motivated not by a romantic conservationism but by the need to delve into tradition in search of innovative and better solutions—that is reflected in the second part of this book, which gathers together a wide set of examples of actual projects inspired by different aspects of the sophisticated Inuit model.

FROM SIBERIA TO GREENLAND

The Inuit people, considered the aboriginal group which has most successfully managed to keep its culture intact in a very wide geographical zone, extends in a sprawling fashion from the northeast of Siberia to the east of Greenland, passing through Alaska and Canada, a region which covers 1,003,870 square miles (2,600,000 km^2). Mostly settled on the coastal strip above the 54°F (12°C) isotherm in August, north of the tree line, the Inuit have traditionally been characterized by a semi-nomadic lifestyle conditioned by the long Arctic winters and based to a great extent on the hunting of marine mammals. Despite the predictable local variations in a territory more than 3,100 miles (5,000 km) wide, the Inuit share the same culture and language, Inuktitut, which has its own alphabet and is spoken by more than 80,000 people.

With a total approximate population of 152,000 members, the Inuit are one of the Arctic communities that have organized politically using their differentiated cultural identity as a starting point. In 1975, the Canadian Inuit, which totals 45,000 people, codified the first law recognizing their right to own and exploit the land, as well as guaranteeing them environmental protection and public services such as schools and hospitals. International interest generated by the great riches of natural gas and oil in the Arctic have led to new agreements between the Inuit and the Canadian government, such as that which led to Nunavut being made an autonomous region in 1993.

An Inuit family building an igloo, Alaska, c. 1924

An Inuit tapestry hung inside a church in Iqualit, Nunavut, Canada

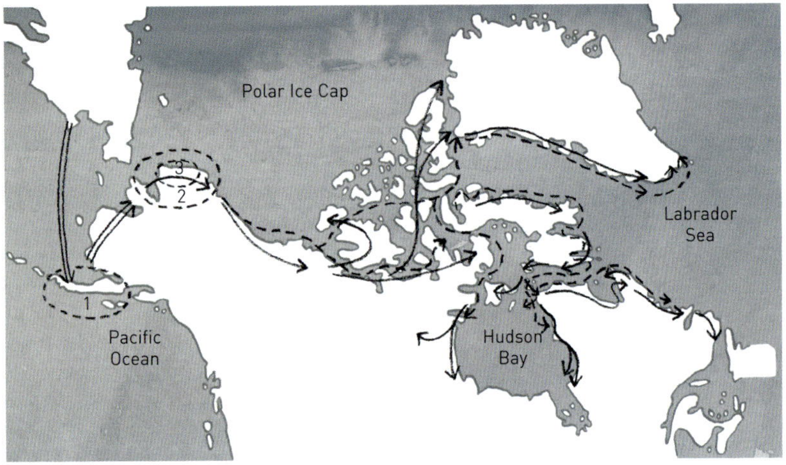

Map of the migration lines and adaptation of the Inuit to the Polar region

Origin of the Siberian east
Sivullirmiut
Taissuman

1 First Inuit territory

2 Development of inland winter adaptation

3 Development of marine hunting and adaptation to the frozen sea

Among the cultural elements shared by the Inuit people are common characteristics in their vernacular architecture, which varies, above all, on available materials. Therefore, the igloo, despite being the Inuit icon par excellence, has traditionally only been used as a winter dwelling in the central area of Canada and in the Thule region of Greenland, whilst in the extreme east and west of the territory (Siberia, Alaska, east of Greenland) it is only used as a temporary hunting shelter.

FIVE THOUSAND YEARS OF HISTORY

Despite being the widespread word used to refer to this Arctic culture, the word Eskimo, a word of Ojibwa origin which probably means "those who eat raw meat," was rejected in favor of Inuit, an Inuktitut term that refers to Indigenous Canadians and can be translated as "we, the people;" in turn, other native peoples of Greenland or Alaska use different names.

As an addendum to this linguistic explanation, it should be said the Inuit do not have any cultural relationship with their Canadian neighbors to the south, the Indians of the First Nations. Five thousand years ago, the ancestors of the Inuit moved from Asia to Alaska across the Bering Strait. From there they spread out until they reached Greenland, during which they developed their knowledge and the habits necessary for survival in an environment of frozen water—hunting marine mammals was the primary source of food. Three cultures developed into the present-day Inuit—Norton, Dorset, and Thule. These groups fixed the routes of seasonal nomadism and perfected survival techniques. Kayaks, harpoons, oil lamps, sleds, and igloos were some of the contributions which they left in their wake.

The first encounters between Europeans and the Inuit did not happen until the sixteenth century, when explorers like Martin Frobisher explored the inhospitable Arctic waters. The initial contact between the indigenous people and the explorers was not exactly cordial, as the episode when Frobisher, arriving at Baffin Island shows: he kidnapped an Inuk and then exhibited him in London as a tourist attraction.

The explorer John Ross discovering polar habitats in 1817, near Cape York, Greenland

An Inuk going inside the corridor of an igloo, *Parry's Diary*, 1821–1823

Two centuries later, and after a mere twenty or so incursions by Europeans spread across time and space, the procession of whalers, furriers, and missionaries began, meaning a change of lifestyle for the Inuit. The introduction of industrial products, such as matches, sugar, and rifles in the everyday life of this people for the first time obliged its members to have money, which they mainly obtained by whale hunting. Once this had lost profitability due to the unsustainable increase in captures, the only sources of cash were the sale of skins from the large scale hunting of the Arctic fox, or doing jobs that did not respect the seasonal cycles of the tradition and social organization of the Inuit in any way. This, among other things, brought about ecological imbalance and the progressive loss of many of the ancestral values, the latter being heightened by the education given in the Christian missions.

If things seem to indicate that the igloo constitutes an evolution of semi-subterranean structures similar to those found in the northeast of Asia, the only certain fact is that this Arctic refuge, whose name originally meant "winter house," was made popular mainly by the Thule culture, ancestors of the Inuit who dedicated themselves to whale hunting. These people, obliged to move along the Arctic coast in search of better hunting, were responsible for spreading a homogenous culture between Alaska and Greenland between 1000 and 1200 A.D. They excelled because of a particular building technique for creating dome-like structures with a partially underground access corridor that was covered in snow to optimize energy efficiency. The results of this influence, which was so widespread in geographical terms and so concentrated in time are the different variations of vernacular architecture found in the region of the Arctic Circle, as will be explained further on.

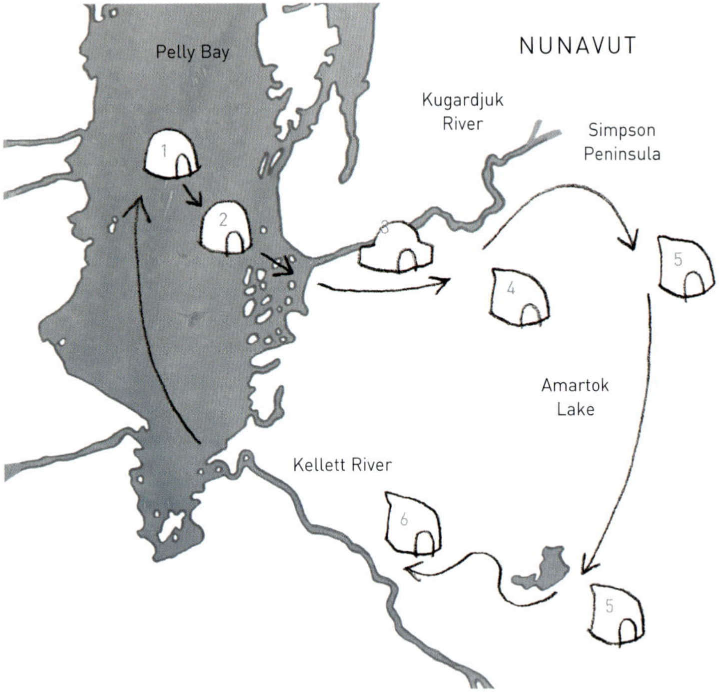

The Inuit shelters varied according to seasonal hunting; in winter they built igloos on the frozen sea, and in the summer they moved to tents situated inland.

1 Mid winter (seal)
2 End of winter (seal)
3 Spring (seal)
4 Mid summer (fish)
5 Beginning of fall (caribou)
6 End of fall (fish)

A stone carving by the indigenous artist Joe Talirunili illustrating the building and hunting patterns according to the seasons of winter or summer, c. 1965

THE FIGHT FOR SURVIVAL

The Arctic is not a pleasant place. Situated above the imaginary line of the Arctic Circle, the Inuit habitat is characterized by barren soil, long months of darkness, strong winds and storms, freezing temperatures, and a scarcity of animals and vegetation. The snow is usually present between October and July, whilst the months of thawing only reveal the permafrost, the surface layer of ground which stays frozen all year and stops the water from penetrating. The scarce vegetation is adapted to the short springs and summers, when the sun does not set. Towards the end of the summer, the colors disappear from the landscape, the birds migrate, and the growing darkness and worsening of the climate make hunting and moving around more difficult.

The hardness of the Arctic climate has radically conditioned the Inuit culture, which is based on a semi-nomadic lifestyle divided between winter and summer, darkness and light, life inside and outside. Traditionally, at the beginning of the winter, great camps of igloos were put up by the edge of the Ocean, as seal hunting constituted the main source of food and fuel. When spring arrived, the population replaced the igloos with tents and spread out to engage themselves in other hunting activities, whilst in the summer they moved inland in a group to follow the caribou and take advantage of the thaw to fish and gather wild fruit, as well as raw materials (plants, drift wood, bones) for their tools. When fall came, they continued to follow the route of the caribou southwards to stockpile provisions and skins in preparation for the winter, this also included repairing sleds, fishing, making clothes, and, alongside this, many family and social gatherings. The semi-nomadic Inuit, forced by the severe climate, required appropriate architecture, quick-to-build igloos and tents and easy-to-take-down-and-transport tents. In an environment with a scarcity of materials and resources, the observation of nature, along with the shelters built by Arctic animals, allowed the Inuit to devel-

An Inuk washing clothes by a summer tent in Alaska, c. 1906

op more sophisticated solutions for their survival; it was then that the igloo became the indisputable protagonist of the Arctic environment.

The cycles of movement by the Inuit have been repeated without variations since the first communities settled in the Arctic and established their routes, which joined the hunting areas on the coast with inland habitats. Each group, whose number of members depended on the availability of resources, followed its own pattern of movements, although on occasion some of them joined together in the summer for large hunting expeditions, or to participate in social celebrations that strengthened the cohesion of the Inuit culture.

Arctic nomadism was possible because of an excellent capacity for orientation on the ice and for identifying the slightest meteorological threats. In addition, other concepts characterize the Inuit culture, like the connection of dependence and intimacy which exists between its members. As the family is the basic unit, there are strong links between the different family nuclei despite living thousands of miles apart. When resources allowed it, the families lived in hamlets of adjacent or connected igloos, joined by a large dome which served as a meeting place. In view of the hostility of the environment, solidarity, hospitality, and sharing became such basic principles of the Inuit way of thinking that individualism came to be viewed as inappropriate behavior. In fact, typical values of nomadic societies included the absence of a state, a social system traditionally based on an equal exchange of goods as well as duties, and a lack of sentiment regarding possession of land. Places are only for passing through, without borders or plots. The absence of divisions in the Inuit nomadic dwellings (the winter igloo or the summer tent), as well as the continuity between the outside and the inside, are particular responses to the formation of a relationship with the environment.

In the last fifty years, the Inuit, like most people with a nomadic tradition, have become progressively more settled. The inhospitable character of their habitat, which kept them isolated from their southern neighbors, has not dissuaded the big mining and oil companies, attracted by the immense richness of resources in the Arctic. The semi-nomadic lifestyle, based on survival ensured by complete communion with nature, is losing ground to a day-to-day sedentary lifestyle governed by an economy of national and commercial interests. The fading subsistence-based lifestyle of the Inuit is thought to be the consequence of these changes and state subsidies as hunting wanes and there are few possibilities of gaining skilled employment, even as the arrogant need to acquire oil and other goods is rampant.

In the field of architecture, the move to a sedentary lifestyle has been linked to the increase in prefabricated housing, totally unsuited for adaptation to the Inuit cultural pattern, and rather inadequate for the Arctic climates, as they lose heat through the floor, cause the permafrost to thaw, and, consequently, sink into the ground. This new addition to the landscape, driven by housing standards which have passed over the characteristic Inuit culture and its familiar shape, has been to the detriment of the igloo, which is hardly used nowadays apart from for hunting trips. In addition, the length of expeditions is reduced as more and more sleds are being replaced by snowmobiles.

Oil pipelines at the Prudhoe Bay refinery in North Slope, Alaska

Inuit children resting by an ATV on a spring day, Pond Inlet, Nunavut, Canada

An Inuk girl learning while playing with a model of an igloo in a school in Igloolik, Nunavut, Canada

The Inuit people, whose isolation over the centuries has allowed them to maintain a strong cultural unity into the twenty-first century, have started to organize and fight to change these rather hopeless prospects. Starting from the premise of conserving and promoting their culture in a compatible way with progress, new education and professional programs have increased the knowledge of traditional skills amongst young people and adults and introduced modern techniques for promoting new business initiatives. In addition, art and traditional craft sectors are growing strongly, which have been organized as carving and engraving cooperatives with great success. Finally, tourism, especially the ecological and cultural varieties are also successful.

If, to their great capacity to adapt, the inhabitants of the Arctic invite optimism, it is also true that the changes seen up till now are possibly not as significant compared to those of the immediate future. The threat of global warming is already a reality throughout the Arctic region, where it is estimated that by the end of the century there will be large areas without ice. The reduction of the ice mass is one of the most dramatic consequences of climate change, as traditional Arctic life completely depends on it. Its reduction has already caused flooding in the coastal villages due to the rise in sea level, as well as the gradual disappearance of the habitat of marine mammals and the shortening of the hunting season due to lack of ice on which to move around. In the short term, the increase in temperatures on the polar ice caps so far has been double that which has occurred in the rest of the world. This means a milder climate with a longer summer which will attract a wider variety of species coming from more southerly areas. However, the scientists are already warning that this poisoned chalice will, in the long term, unbalance the delicate ecosystem, as well as destabilize the sled trail. All these changes will transform the Arctic landscape and oblige its inhabitants to become involved, again, in the fight for survival.

Step by step: the construction of an igloo

BLOCK BY BLOCK

Despite its reduced presence in the modern Inuit world as a result of the decline of hunting and the gradual move to a sedentary society, the igloo continues to be a basic element of the Inuit of central Canada. The construction of this winter shelter is usually the responsibility of the men, normally two, a layer and a cutter, or one, if it is a small igloo. Women and children traditionally adopt the role of helpers, giving the final touches to the shape. In the building process, the participation of different generations is fundamental, as passing down skills from father to son is one of the basic characteristics of this type of architecture.

The size of the igloo varies according to its intended function: from 7 feet (2 meters) in diameter for temporary shelters, to 15 feet (4.5 meters) for more permanent structures. An able builder can complete a simple igloo in an hour, but a semi-permanent family dwelling can take longer.

The first key factors in the construction of an igloo are the position and the quality of the snow. The best option is to position it on a terrain sloping slightly to the south or towards the east, to avoid the prevailing winds. The slope means that the storms will accumulate snow at the back of the igloo (always facing east or south), which improves its insulation, although a nearby cliff or protective parapet can stand in for the slope. To find animals for hunting more easily, especially marine mammals, the igloo is often positioned on the accumulated snow on the frozen sea. After choosing its location,

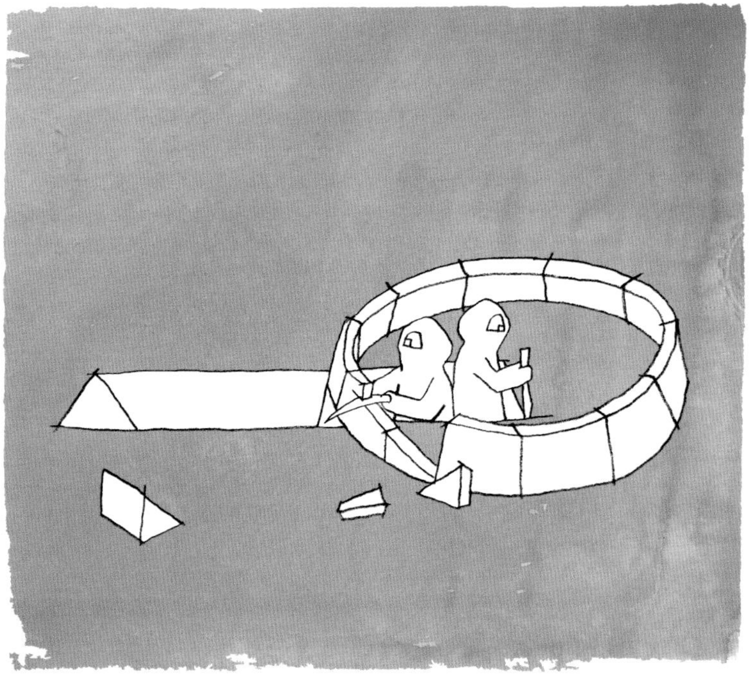

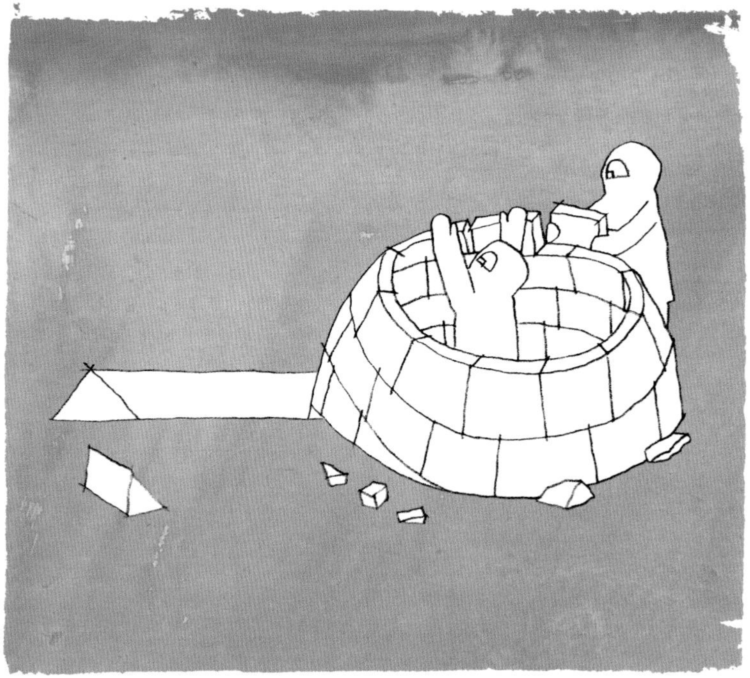

a probe is usually used to test the consistency of the snow, which, due to its high insulating capacity, is an excellent material for building. The snow must be sufficiently malleable to be able to be cut with a curved knife, *orsulung*, (according to tradition it is made of bone or caribou antlers), but never too soft or grainy, as then the blocks will crumble. The probe, a long thin piece of bone, antler, or wood, is sunk into the ground: if it goes down smoothly then the snow is even, firm, and from a single snowfall. This last characteristic is essential: if different layers are used, the blocks could come apart. For a medium size igloo, made of thirty or forty blocks, it is necessary to check an amount of snow that is the equivalent to the diameter of the igloo plus a meter deep. If there is a lack of good snow, then this can be compensated for by building a narrower, taller structure which will give more stability.

Once the location and the material have been checked, the builder can draw a circle the size of the floor of the igloo in the snow. From this, two separated parallel lines are drawn. The distance between these lines is the length that the block of snow should be (between 2 and 3.25 feet [60 and 100 cm]). Between the two lines, the cutter extracts blocks that are 1 foot to 2 feet (30 to 60 cm) tall and between 4 and 6 inches (10 and 15 cm) deep. This creates a corridor that provides access to the interior of the igloo. Halfway down the corridor and coinciding with the outline of the circle, the first block is placed, and then the others one by one, leaning slightly inwards around the initial circle until the first row is complete. This is cut on the cross so that the layer can continue building the wall in a spiral. Lastly, the final block is fixed from the inside, fixing the upper part of the dome, and an access route is created by making an opening in

the first block inserted in the initial corridor. This is situated lower than the floor of the igloo to prevent cold air from coming in; it is covered with snow to turn it into an access point.

The building is completed and adapted to the needs of each family. The women and children fill the gaps between the blocks with snow and cover the interior of the dome with another layer of compacted snow with the help of some wooden shovels. Once this has frozen, this snow serves to finish sealing the structure. Over the access door a window is opened up, covered with a piece of freshwater ice or animal intestine, and higher up another hole is made to ventilate the igloo. In front of the door, another dome structure is constructed, which serves as a porch, while, according to the needs of the family, other secondary igloos are placed against it to serve as a larder, doghouse, or washroom. Next to the kitchen area, a small annex is added for caribou meat and skin, to make sure they stay frozen and do not go rotten. Given the hospitality of the Inuit, the dwellings need to be flexible to be able to house unexpected guests. Therefore, from a single igloo a series of domes intersecting with the first one can be built, opening or omitting the shared wall, to transform a structure for one family into a small community of three, four, or five interconnected igloos that can house up to twenty people. These structures often add up to a larger scale igloo, the *kashim*, used to celebrate festivals and gatherings.

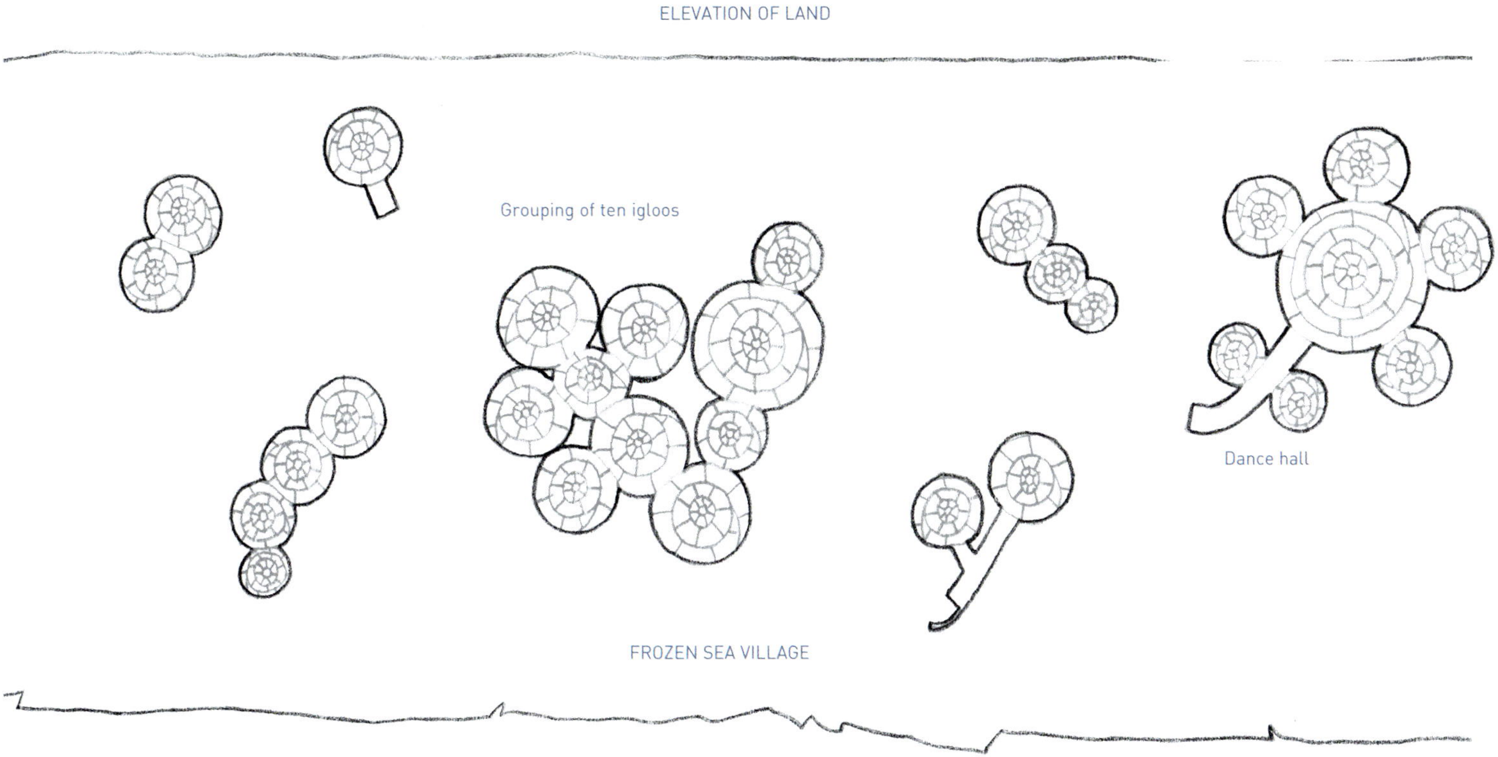

Possible groupings of igloos

Taboos and superstitions, which are very significant in the Inuit culture, also govern the process of building an igloo. According to tradition, to guarantee good luck, the first blocks to be extracted are the blocks destined for the "long side" (the side connected to the door) and afterwards those of the "wide side" (rear part of the igloo). Likewise, if a couple would like a large family, the first block of the wide side has to be cut with a serrated knife, and for the children to have good luck, all the loose pieces of snow on the floor have to be removed. Lastly, to ensure easy births, the upper opening where the key block is fitted to close the dome must be especially wide.

The construction technique of the igloo varies in the details and finishes according to the toughness of the climate and the availability of fuel. Also, the availability of other materials, such as wood, stone, or whale bones, has generated variations of the winter shelter across the vast Arctic territory, such as the Alaskan *anegiuchak*, which has snow walls and a square floor covered in tiles on which snow is flattened, or the *killegun*, made of blocks of snow which encircle a canvas tent.

Floor Plan

1 Entrance
2 Platform
3 Meat storage
4 Lamp with grill above

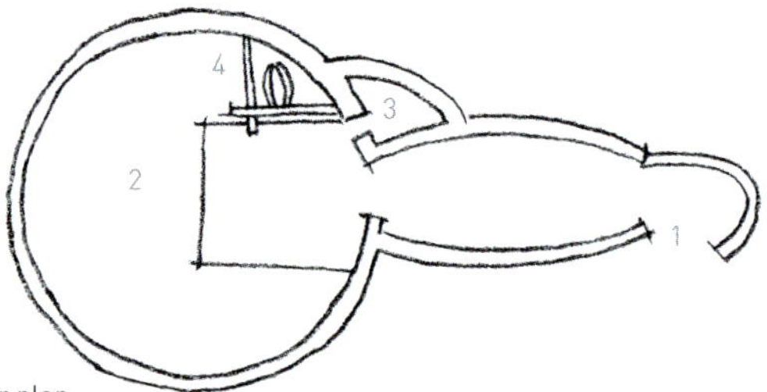

Floor plan

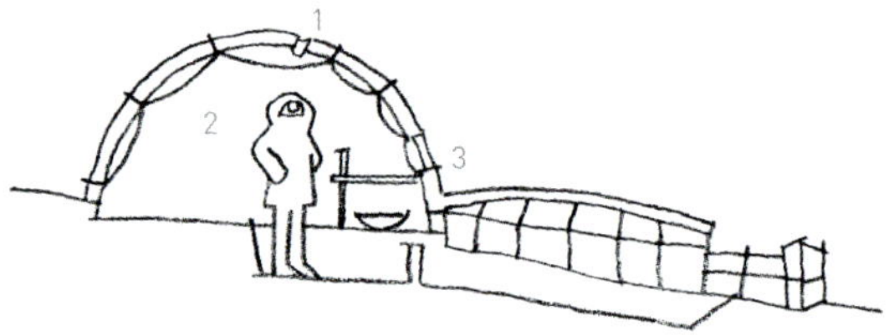

Cross section

1 Opening for ventilation
2 Interior coverings with skins
3 Window

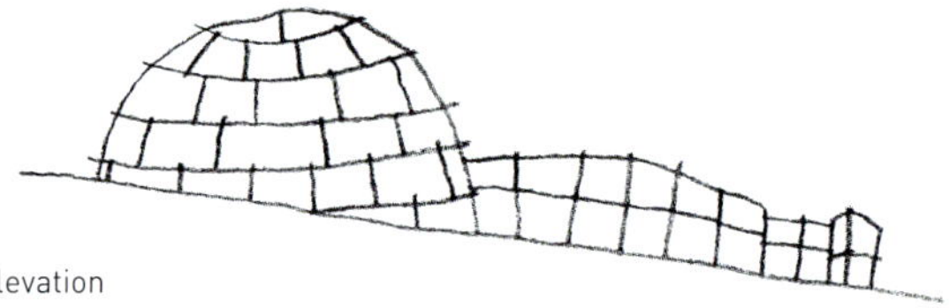
Elevation

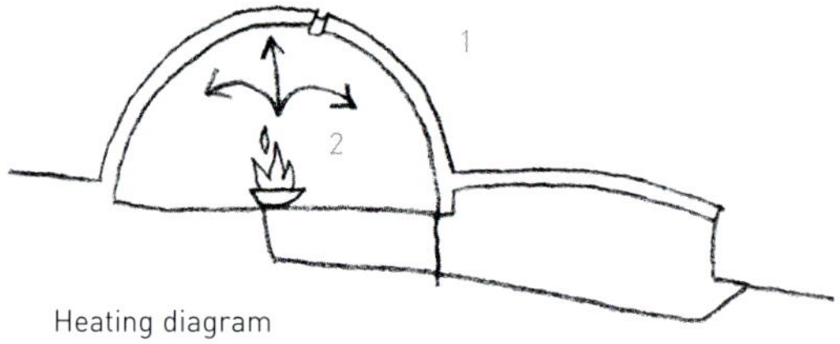

Heating diagram

1 Cold air
2 Hot air

EFFICIENCY ABOVE ALL

If efficiency is the inherent characteristic of all vernacular structures, in an environment as inhospitable as the Arctic, this quality is absolutely essential to ensure the survival of its inhabitants. Faced with an extreme scarcity of resources, the Inuit found inspiration in nature for building their own winter refuge: just like the animals and the plants, the inhabitants of the igloo use the insulating capacity of the snow to modify the climate inside their shelter. However, building a long lasting, hard-wearing, and adaptable dwelling with this material requires a long process of trial and error that ends in a simple and perfect catenary dome. For one thing, the dome is one of the most efficient structures, as it gives the maximum volume with the minimum surface, it is quick to build, easy to heat, and offers minimum resistance to the wind and the cold. In contrast to the semi-sphere, its catenary shape does not require any extra support due to the optimum height-diameter relationship.

After completing the construction and with the aim of fixing the structure permanently, an oil lamp is lit inside so that the hot air begins to melt the blocks of snow, immediately afterwards cold air is let in to the dome and it freezes again instantly. In this way, the blocks stay firmly joined to each other and to the ground and can bear the weight of an adult. This also allows for part of the igloo to be destroyed to add extensions, thus guaranteeing its versatility. The use of snow as the only material also makes this type of vernacular construction an example of sustainable building, as it uses renewable resources and, with the arrival of spring, it disappears without a trace.

Together with resistance and sustainability, efficient energy is another of the strong points of this structure developed by the Thule culture. The system is based on the principle of capturing air, that is: the igloo is an inverted container that captures the warm air, which tends to rise. To do this, the entrance tunnel is dug at a lower level than the living area which, in turn, has a platform which is elevated even higher, designed to be the bedroom. Added to this basic law of physics are

Drawing of the inside of an igloo in Alaska, c.1916

Avataq, an Inuk hunter dressed in polar bear skin pants, lights a stove inside an igloo. Northeast Greenland

other simple but ingenious techniques that help to maintain a rather comfortable temperature inside the dwelling, as will be explained in the next chapter.

HOME, SWEET HOME

Once the men have finished the basic structure of the dome, the women are in charge of organizing the interior, whose shape mirrors the rituals set by the Inuit culture. Through a hole made in the wall, which will later be covered, all the furniture and fittings are brought into the igloo. Next the inner walls are covered with caribou or seal skins which are sewn together to make a layer to trap the air which insulates against the cold and stops the dripping when the ceiling blocks melt.

The living area of the igloo, which is reached through a door 3 feet (90 cm) high, is divided into two unequal parts: the *natiq*, nearer to the door, for general use, and the *iqliq*, the bedroom-living room which occupies two thirds of the living space. In the *natiq*, a square part of the floor is situated next to the access tunnel and at the same level; it is used as an entrance hall and storage area. On three of its four sides it is bordered by the *iqliq*, a platform of snow between 2.5 and 3 feet (75 and 90 cm) high covered with moss or branches and skins used for sitting, sleeping and eating. According to Inuit mythology, the *natiq* is related to the masculine world, to men's tools and the sea, whilst the *iqliq* is linked to women, their tools and the earth.

One of the basic items that the Inuit carry in the sled is an oil lamp or *kuliq*, which men generally carve from soapstone or tailor's chalk (a type of talc) and then give to women as a gift. Used to give heat and light, the lamp has the shape of an oval tray about 1 to 3.25 feet (30 to 100 cm) long; at the bottom a wick dipped in animal fat burns slowly. Above the lamp, on a platform to the right of the *natiq*, a structure is placed for the cooking pot or kettle, both made of soapstone, and above these a rack is hung for drying clothes and shoes.

Between the lamp, whose effect is multiplied by the reflection on the frozen walls, and human heat, the temperature in the igloo can exceed 32°F (0°C) when temperatures outside are -40°F

(-40 °C). But life was harder for the Inuit that lived further from the coast and lacked any type of fuel. To adjust the temperature, the opening of the chimney was partially blocked, making it necessary to keep an eye on the flame of the lamp, which showed the need for more ventilation by changing color.

The platform, or *iqliq* was the main stage for Inuit life during the winter. Throughout the day each member of the family, composed of a couple and their offspring, carried out their corresponding tasks on the platform, which was turned into a communal bed at night. Curiously, in this tight family relationship there is hardly any room for intimacy and the domestic divisions which characterize the modern world. This conditioning creates a challenge for the Inuit who have had to adopt a sedentary life in their new standard houses designed with a separate space for each activity.

The igloos designed for living in have an average life of a month—often the walls suffer the effects of family life or the inhabitants decide to move in search of better hunting. In spring, what has been a warm winter home becomes an uncomfortable place to live, as the walls, turned to ice by the changes in temperature, are continually dripping and lose their capacity to insulate against the cold. When not even the patches of dry snow can stop the dripping, it is time to move to the transition home or *qarmaq*, a circular structure of blocks of ice or snow covered with canvas, or a tent set up inside this structure. In summer the *tupiq* or tent, made from canvas or skins and a structure of interlaced willow branches or antlers is ideal for hunting expeditions, whilst in the fall the *qarmaq* is used again, as it offers protection from the first cold spells before the snow has a good enough quality to be able to build an igloo again.

The Inuit community of the Arctic Bay on the north coast of Baffin Island, Nunavut, Canada

The old Catholic church in Igloolik made of stone, c. 1960, Nunavut, Canada

The modern church in Kópavogur, a suburb of Reykjavik, Iceland

THE FUTURE OF THE IGLOO

For many years vernacular architecture has been considered an unchanging model which was studied particularly for its aesthetic and decorative value. More recently, the environmental and cultural context which shapes vernacular architecture has come to the forefront. Change forms part of this discipline, as its strong link with the environment obliges it to adapt or disappear. For the Inuit, the type of semi-nomadic lifestyle in which only an igloo could guarantee survival is being gradually stamped out. Today, used only for hunting expeditions, this model is on the verge of disappearing, although its influence continues to be present in Inuit families who adapt their dwellings to continue carrying out tasks in the same shared space. The Inuit building technique is also visible today in hybrid buildings, structures between modernity and tradition, such as self-built houses, which combine waste materials with earth, stone, or snow. In the last few years, the recognition of the vernacular has become a weapon brandished against the specter of globalization, which threatens to put an end to difference and anything local. Nevertheless, in the case of the igloo, such recognition has often been limited to imitation of its forms, without studying the functional nature of the structure, its sophisticated efficiency, or the knowledge of the environment that it requires. New architectural trends have started to finally choose to delve into the deep meaning of the igloo with very disparate results, which are shown in the second part of this book.

FROM VERNACULAR TO CONTEMPORARY

MANY ARCHITECTS TODAY
HAVE BEEN INSPIRED,
CONSCIOUSLY OR SUBCONSCIOUSLY,
BY THE TRADITIONAL IGLOO
FOR THE DESIGN OF SOME OF
THEIR RECENT WORKS.
THE FOLLOWING PAGES GATHER TOGETHER
A SELECTION OF PROJECTS,
DESIGNED BY LOCAL ARCHITECTS
AS WELL AS FAMOUS INTERNATIONAL FIGURES,
WHO IN SOME WAY
REFLECT OR REINTERPRET
CHARACTERISTICS OF
THIS ANCIENT ANCESTRAL STRUCTURE.

The pictograms shown here are used to quickly identify the way the vernacular igloo has been interpreted; the new structure could use the shape of the original igloo, the building process, its material, or even a combination of these characteristics. Therefore one or more of these pictograms are included at the beginning of each project with the aim of helping to identify the nature of each interpretation.

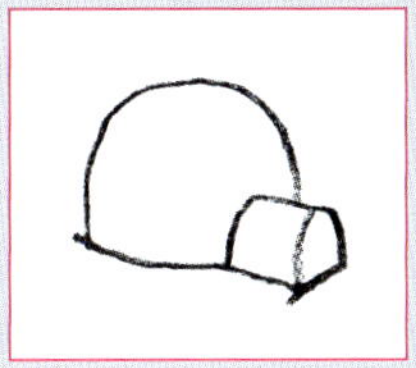

SHAPE The vault in the form of a half-sphere offers the maximum volume possible to the minimum occupied surface. Its outline also helps the conservation of heat inside.

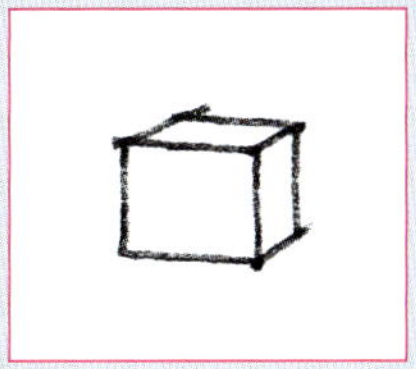

MATERIAL In the Arctic landscape, ice is the only dominant resource—it is also the most efficient material. Its insulating character offers excellent protection against outside temperatures.

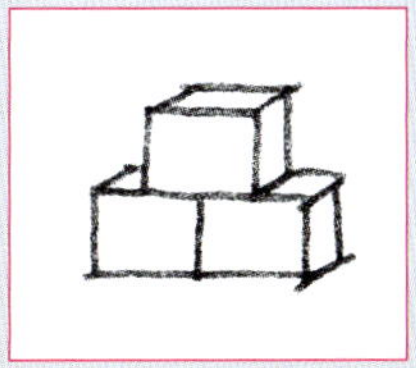

BUILDING PROCESS The laying of beveled blocks in the form of a spiral facilitates the creation of a self-standing structure, which also prevents its collapse whilst it is being built.

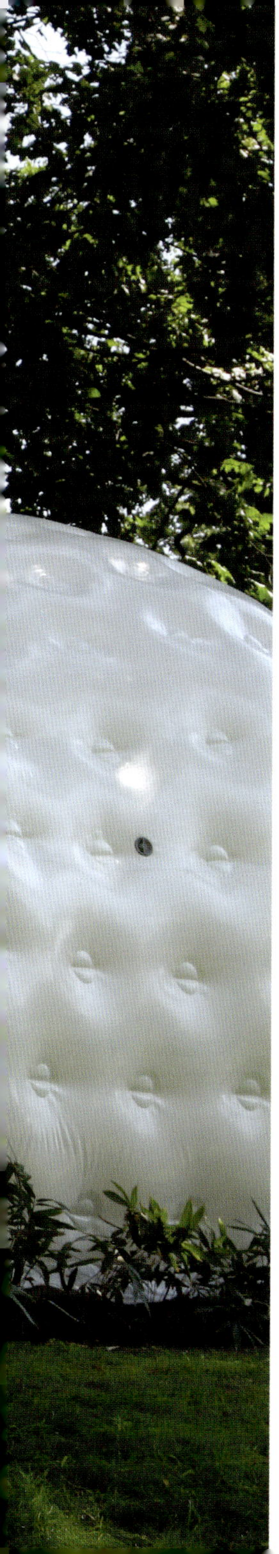

TEA HOUSE

ARCHITECT Kengo Kuma & Associates
LOCATION Frankfurt, Germany

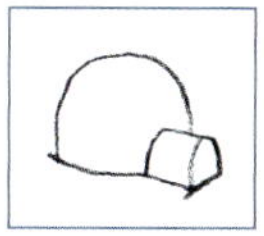

TYPE OF PROJECT Pavilion
AREA 333 ft^2 (31 m^2)
HEIGHT 8 ft (2.5 m)
DURATION OF CONSTRUCTION 3 months
YEAR OF COMPLETION 2007
PHOTOS © Museum Applied Art Frankfurt

Reverence, harmony, purity and tranquility.

With the intention of projecting these four concepts, the architects have reworked the ancient Japanese tea house with an avant-garde design based on an air structure. The architects wanted to go one step further than the inert buildings of the twentieth century and create a dynamic installation that breathes to the same rhythm as its environment: the Museum for Applied Art Frankfurt.

In terms of the technique, a double membrane made from an innovative fabric called tenara was used with air inserted. Both layers are connected by a polyester thread, which is joined together in joins every 24 inches (600 mm), as can be seen from the outside of the installation. The tenara has a fiberglass base and, therefore, has a soft, light, almost transparent texture that is hanging by a thread between the real world and the imaginary world.

The double membrane which composes the pneumatic structure is shown by the modeling of the joins, in the form of buttons, visible from the outside.

Traditional tatami mats are spread around the interior to make adjustments for the ritual preparations. The asymmetrical shape of the Tea House is not accidental. Its ethereal exterior recalls the purity of an igloo, as well as the crossed ventilation system which keeps the interior comfortable.

Architecture that breathes deeply ennobles its own space, whilst that which contains the air impoverishes it.

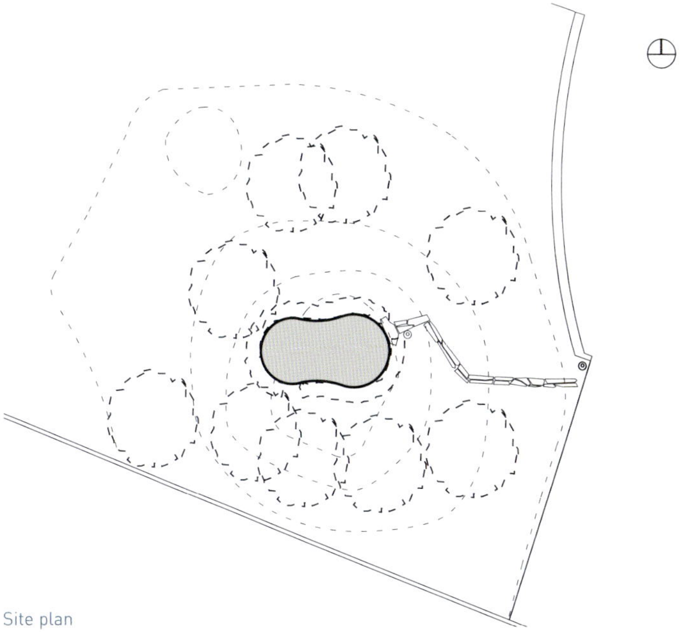

Site plan

Versatility, the ephemeral character of the construction, and its proportions evoke the architectural qualities of the traditional igloo.

The dynamic architecture created by Kengo Kuma & Associates is opposed to the choked constructions of the metropolis. With this project the technical principles of the vernacular igloo are saved and its relevance will last through time. It is a room of a single shell that shelters humanity, physically as well as spiritually, in the minimum amount of space, without inhibiting breathing.

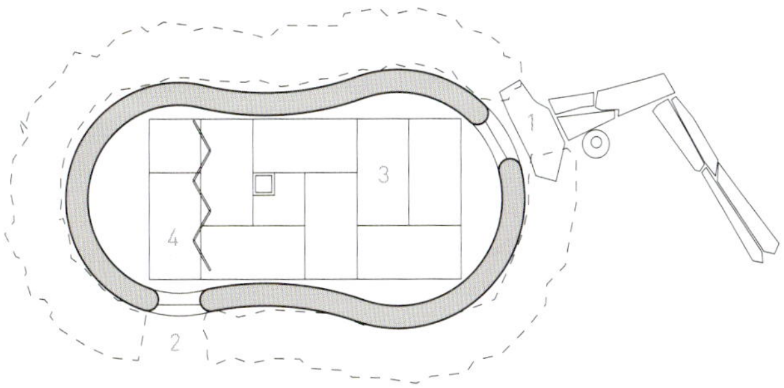

Floor plan

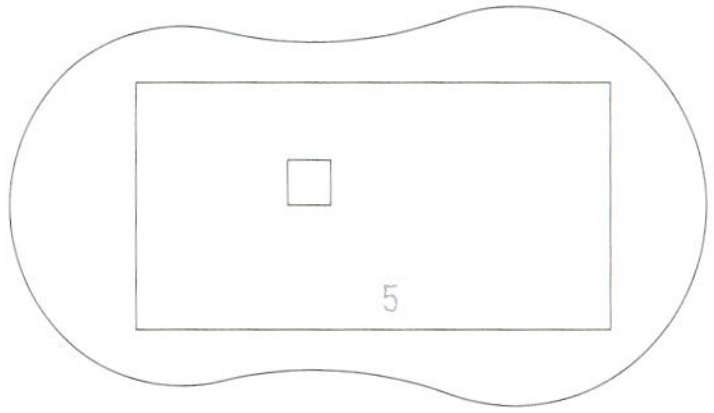

Concrete base

1 Main entrance
2 Service entrance
3 Tea House
4 Preparation area
5 Concrete foundations

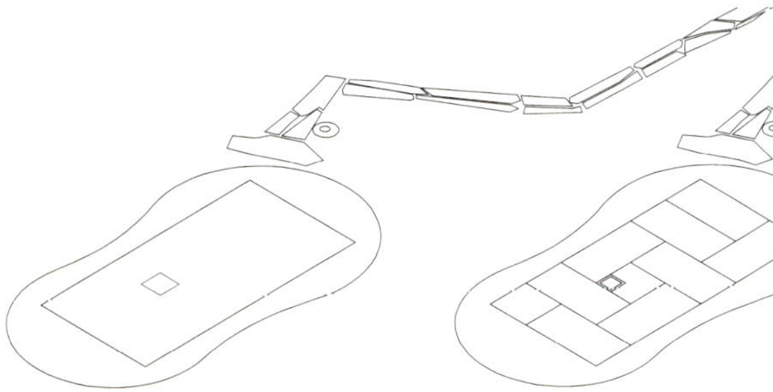

Foundation plan

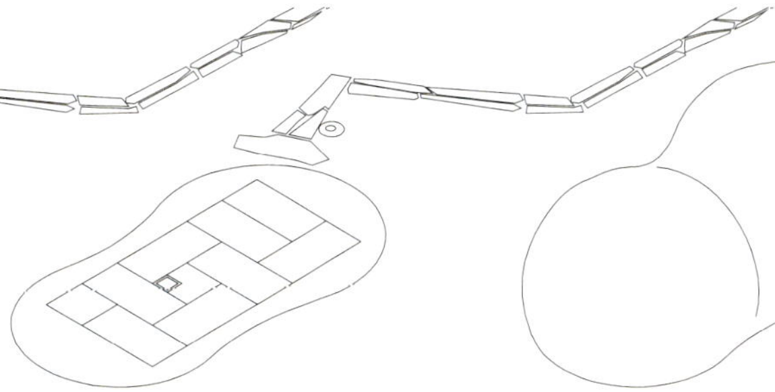

Tatami mat floor

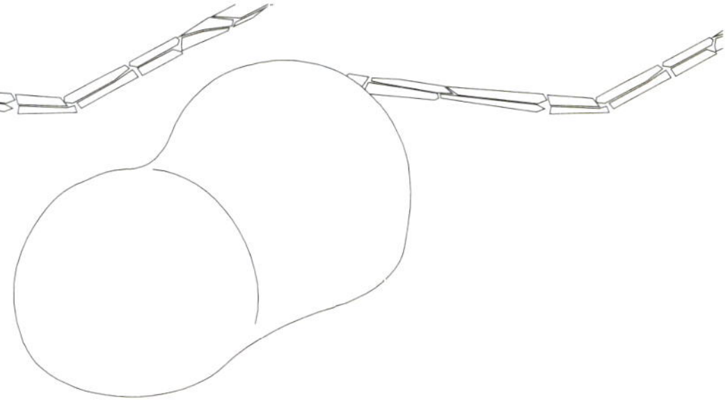

Inflatable membrane

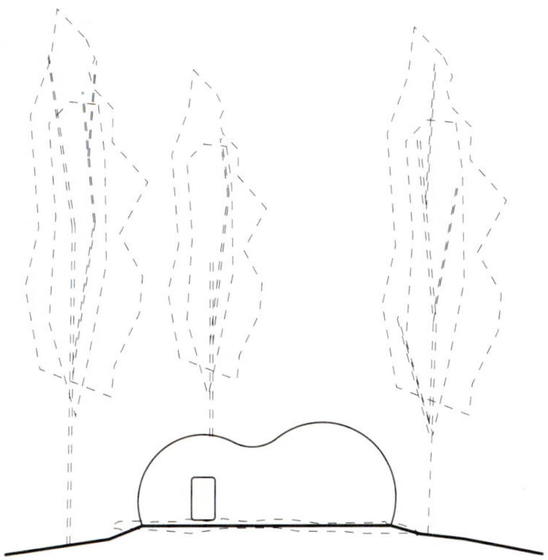

Side elevation

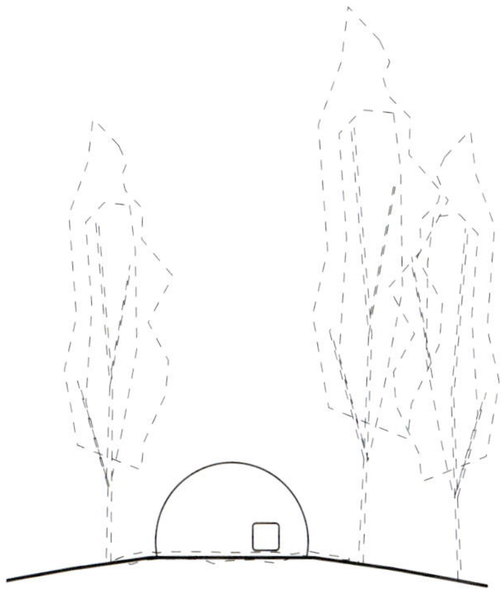

Front elevation

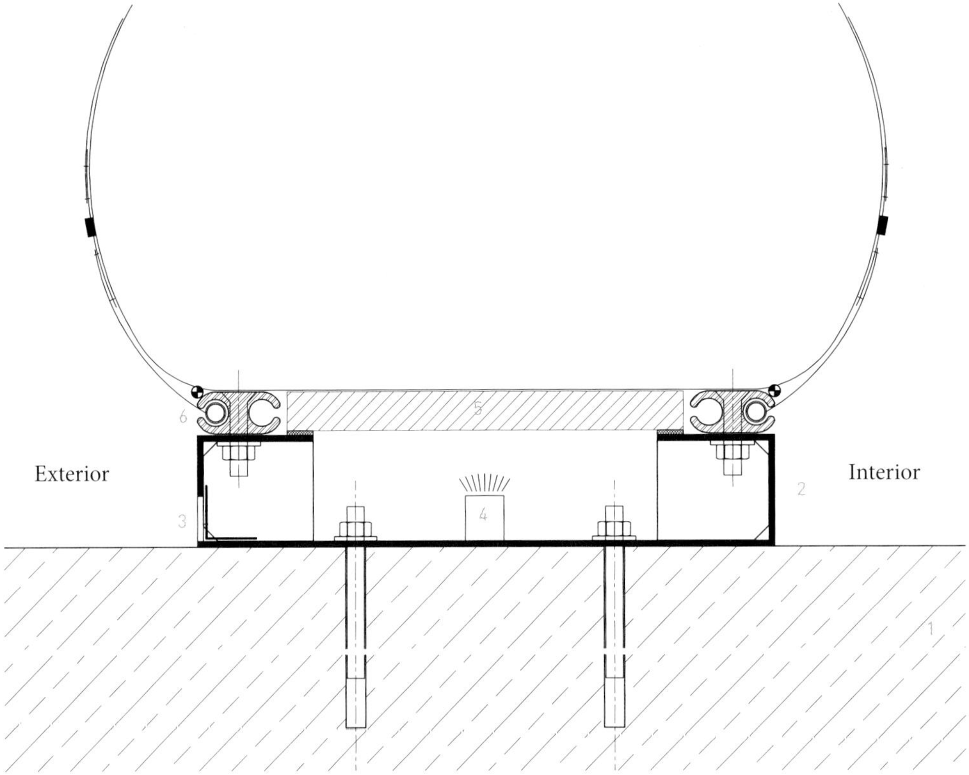

1 Concrete base
2 Metal frame
3 Drainage hole
4 LED lighting
5 Tatami mat Platforms
6 Aluminum side

Detail of the connection between the membrane and the base

INTERVIEW WITH **KENGO KUMA**

> THE FACT THAT SUCH A DELICATE SKIN CAN PROTECT SOMETHING AS FRAGILE AS THE HUMAN BODY AGAINST EXTREME CONDITIONS IS TRULY SURPRISING.

What concepts inspired this project?
Many things inspired me, including the traditional igloo. It is a form which is strongly linked to ancient Japanese houses.

How do you relate vernacular architecture to your work?
Vernacular architecture respects the human body, and my architecture is also based on the human body.

What can we learn from vernacular architecture, and specifically from the igloo?
It is free and remains independent from a Cartesian model. It doesn't use materials like concrete and steel and this gives us many clues. The softness of the skin of the igloo, for example, generates a sensation of comfort for its guests, and this made me reflect on the texture of the covering.

Why do you believe that the igloo has become such a cherished icon of the home?
The human body is extremely fragile, and therefore it needs to be protected by a skin with a soft texture like the igloo. And the fact that such a delicate skin can protect something as fragile as the human body against extreme conditions is truly surprising.

MEMORIAL MONUMENT TO THE VICTIMS OF 11-M

ARCHITECT Estudio FAM
LOCATION Madrid, España

TYPE OF PROJECT Memorial monument
AREA 4,040 ft^2 [375 m^2] (cylinder), 5,382 ft^2 [500 m^2] (interior room)
HEIGHT 36 ft (11 m)
DURATION OF CONSTRUCTION 17 months
YEAR OF COMPLETION 2007
PHOTOS © Esaú Acosta

A few meters from the scene of the terror, at the Atocha Station in Madrid, is the memorial monument to honor the 191 victims who were killed in the terrorist attack on March 11, 2004. The architects of FAM have designed this architectural tribute with all solemnity, respect, and sensibility required by a project of this magnitude.

At the heart of the station a cylinder of glass weighing 140 tons rises up 36 ft (11 m) above the ground, finishing in an oval shape without using a single gram of steel. In the underground part of the monument, there is a room housing thousands of messages of condolence from the people of the city engraved in a translucent EFTE membrane. It receives the sunlight at dawn and dusk every day, extolling the unity of the column of glass. It is a simple form with 15,000 curvilinear blocks of borosilicate piled up, made of piec-

es which are convex on one side and concave on the other, joined by a simple compression method based on a logical and natural system. This building technique is similar to that of the igloo, but put together with the latest technological advances. The secret of this achievement lies in the innovative, transparent adhesive that is used to solder together the blocks of solid glass, even in adverse weather conditions such as those in

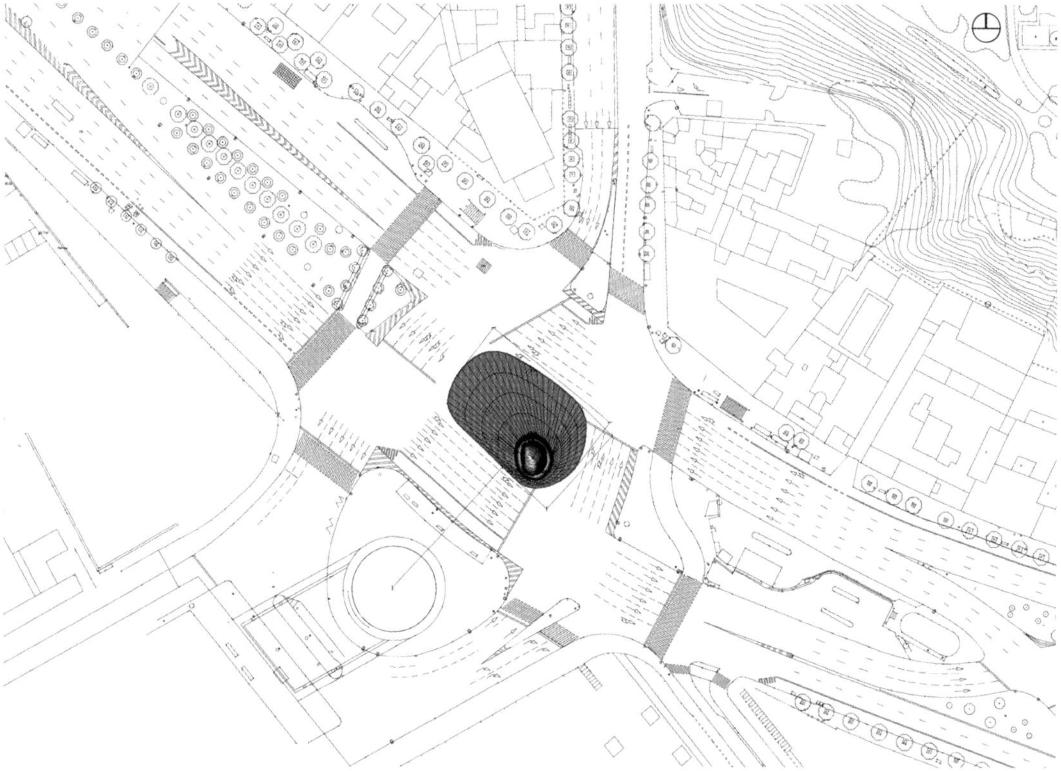

Site plan

The monumental character of the project comes, to a great extent, from its location, at the crossroads of four main roads of the city.

1 Entrance
2 Exit
3 Main room

Floor plan

Elevation

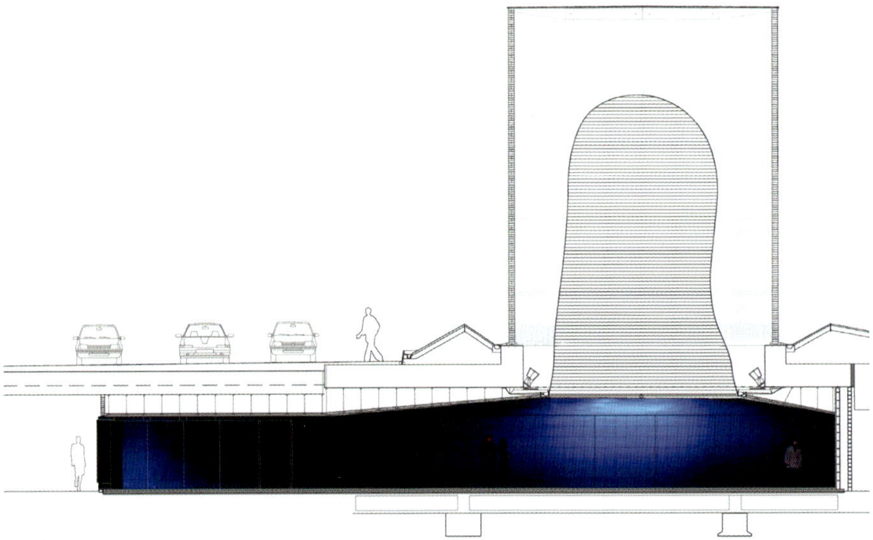

Cross section

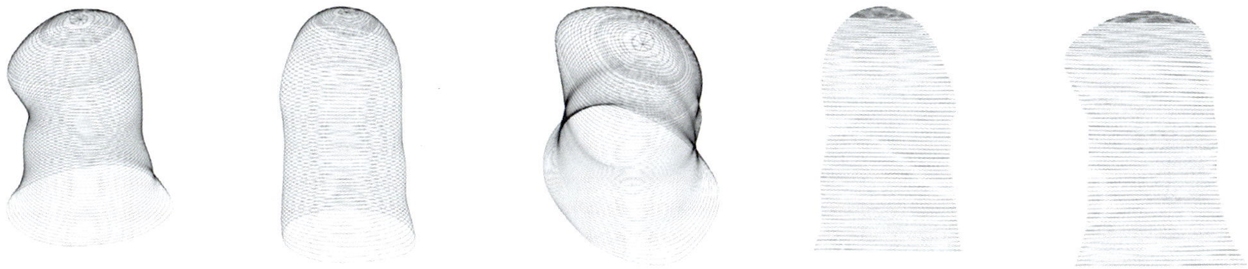

Axonometric studies of the interior form of the cylinder

Madrid. The joints of the structure as well as the messages on life and death engraved on the walls of the cylinder are visible whilst walking in the street. The phenomenon reaches its fullest sense of meaning from inside. Rays of light come in contact with the column in a different way each day, focusing on a different message according to the time, meaning that the monument itself plays an active part in this homage.

General plan of the cylinder

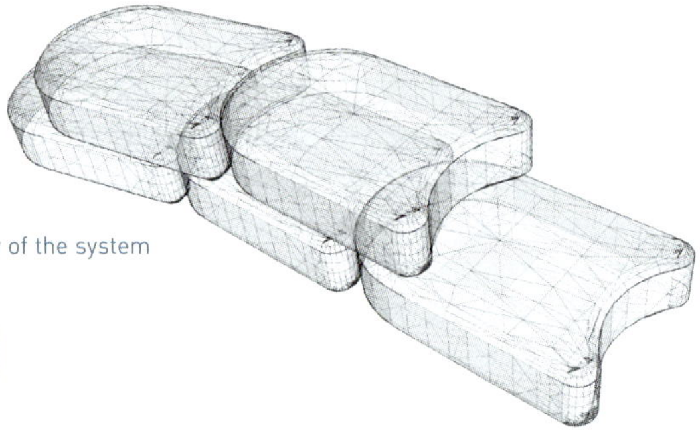

3D view of the system

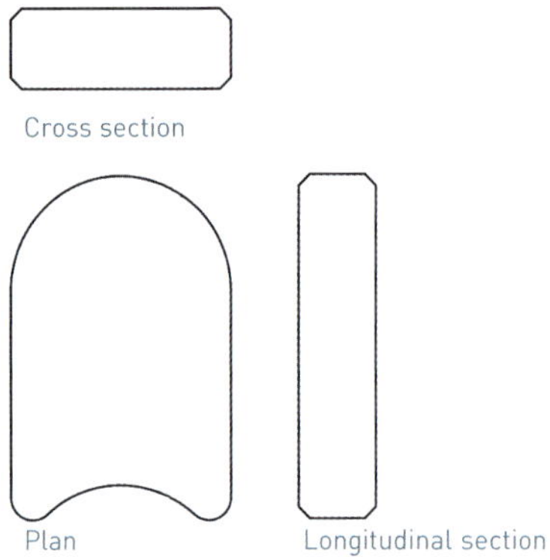

Details of a piece of the glass

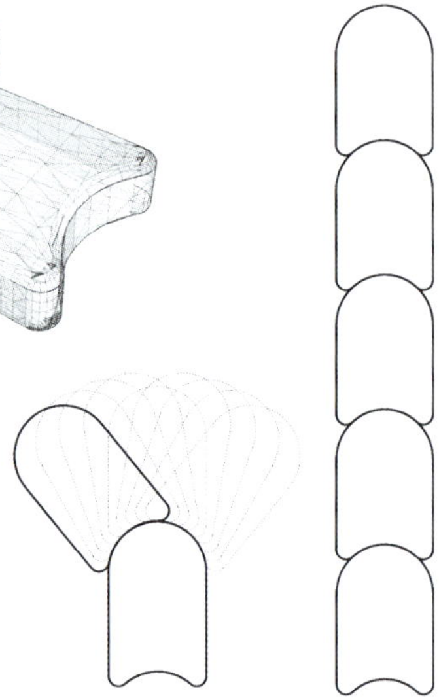

Ball and socket system

> THE IDEA OF PROTECTING YOURSELF IN SUCH A HOSTILE ENVIRONMENT USING THE CHARACTERISTICS OF THE MATERIALS OF THE PLACE MEANS MAKING THE PROBLEM INTO A SOLUTION.

Was the igloo a source of inspiration for this project?

Since the beginning of this project, the igloo represented a valuable source of inspiration, as we wanted to construct a building 11 m high only out of glass which closed above our heads, without using steel. We wanted to obtain the most volume in the smallest possible area. Also, we wanted to use a single material such as glass bonded with glue. You can link the final solution to the natural way that an igloo is built. A high-tech project with curves and other elements wasn't developed; it was decided to work with simple compression, with the pure and simple method of applying one glass on top of another. Just like walls used to be built in villages.

What values of this typology have you wanted to reflect with this monument?

The studio is always interested in the vernacular because of the need to make things in a natural and logical way. It seems that the vernacular normally hides the reason behind something having one form or another. It appears natural rather than pompous. This idea is reflected in the monument. The walls of the glass cylinder don't show the most important element of the project: the joints and the form of the piece. Any question about how the building stands up is answered by these two elements and, yet, they cannot be seen from the outside. In the joints, all the effort and all the research of two years of development in the lab is concentrated. It can be called "high-tech."

What can be learned from vernacular architecture?

For us one of the most important values of vernacular architecture is the implicit desire for the buildings to go unnoticed and react to the conditions of the context. It is this architecture without an architect which should be valued more in the very media-driven age that we live in.

Why do you believe that the igloo has become an icon so closely linked to vernacular dwellings?

We believe that the naturalness with which an igloo is conceived, the idea of protecting yourself in such a hostile environment using the characteristics of the materials of the place means making the problem into a solution, as it manages to warm a volume of air with ice.

ICEHOTEL

ARCHITECT Åke Larsson
LOCATION Jukkasjärvi, Sweden

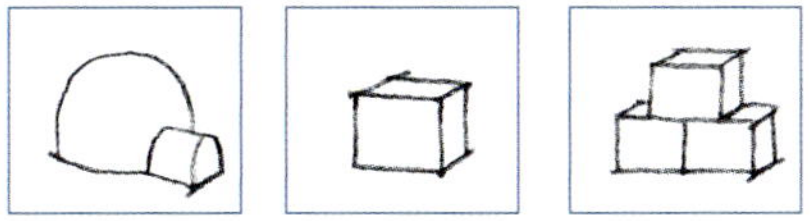

TYPE OF PROJECT Hotel
AREA 7,535 ft^2 (700 m^2)
DURATION OF CONSTRUCTION 2 month
YEAR OF COMPLETION 1990 First version (rebuilt each year)
PHOTOS © Arctic-images/Arcticphoto.com for Ragnar Siggurdssen

On the banks of the River Torne you can find the small Swedish village of Jukkasjärvi, around 125 miles (200 km) from the Arctic Circle. Year after year a team of designers, artists, and architects build a new version of this romantic building. The team avails itself of the natural raw material of the Swedish winter to build a building that synchronizes its calendar with that of nature. The process starts in the middle of November when the snow falls on the giant steel molds that sustain the structure. After a few days the shape becomes rigid and the artificial supports can be removed. Construction consists of five phases: each time a section is ready, it opens its doors to the public, whilst the rest is still under construction. The first phase is completed around December 7 and each week a new part is opened until approximately January 5, when the

hotel is completely finished. The labyrinthine corridors are divided into arched rooms. The domes shine like cut diamonds. Artists the world over do not want to miss the opportunity to demonstrate their work made of ice. From their inspiration, extraordinary designs are born which lift the igloo to the category of pure luxury.

However, the origin of the igloo was simpler, and was only an efficient search for a protective shelter from the cold; however, its simplicity did not mean it was any less technical. The quality of the snow was a fundamental factor in the traditional dwellings of the Inuit. It is just as important in this symbol reinvented by the modern world, in which the material used for art and for the architecture of the structure comes directly from the flow of the crystal waters of the River Torne, capable of making the purest ice.

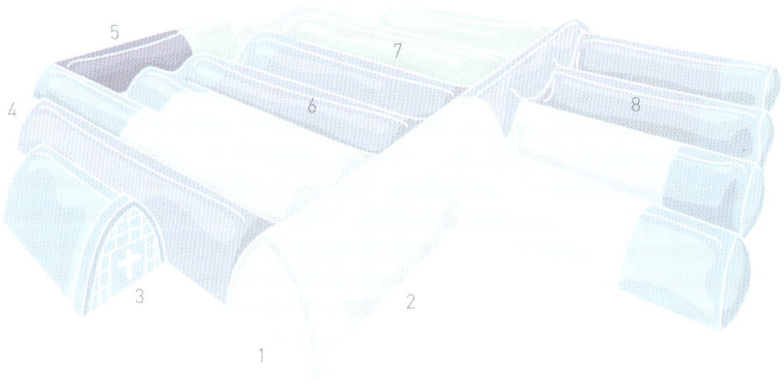

Overall axonometric view

1 Entrance
2 Reception
3 Chapel
4 Bar
5 Luxury suite
6 Art suites
7 Design suites
8 Rooms

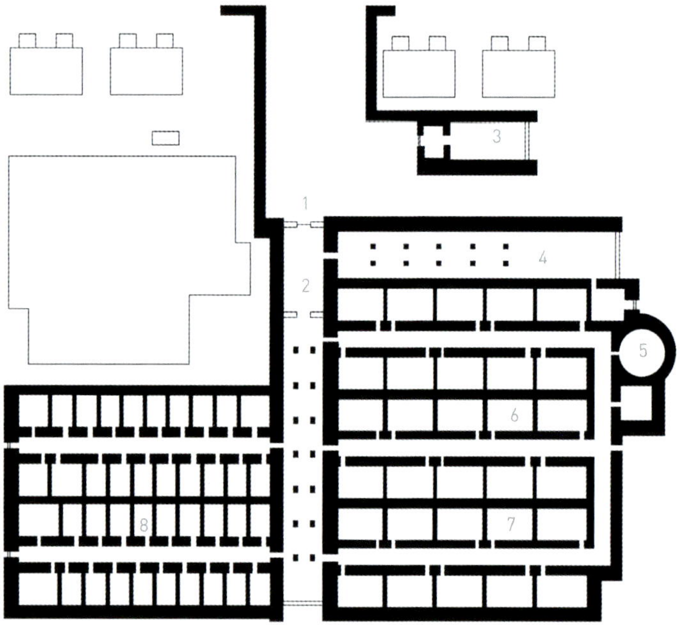

General plan

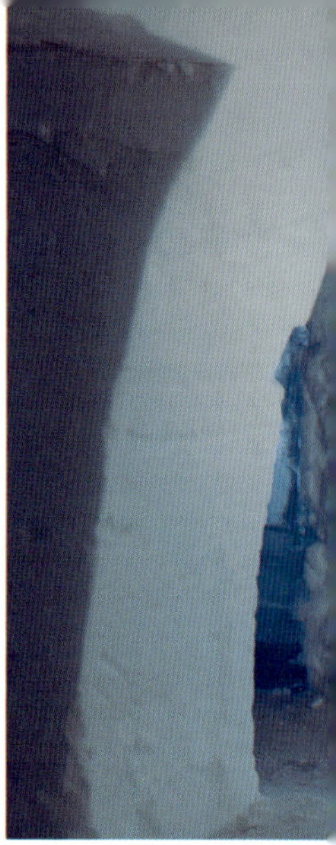

THE OCA

ARCHITECT Königsberger Vannucchi Arquitectura
LOCATION São Paulo, Brazil

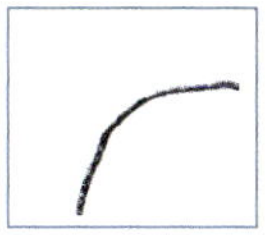

YPE OF PROJECT Pavilion
AREA 3,488 ft^2 (324 m^2)
HEIGHT 15 ft (4.5 m)
DURATION OF CONSTRUCTION 15 days
YEAR OF COMPLETION 2004
PHOTOS © Gal Oppido

Inspired by the traditional Brazilian indigenous houses from which this pavilion takes its name, the Oca was developed as a center of discussion about the native cultures of different communities in the country, built as part of the 2004 World Forum of Cultures in Sao Paulo. It is a meeting place in which various activities can take place: from ceremonies to meetings organized by the architects.

The project uses typical elements of indigenous native architecture such as lighting through a skylight or a high level of transparency in the construction, but without being just a reproduction of this type of vernacular architecture. It also incorporates contemporary elements such as sheets of galvanized steel, which gives the structure more body. The pavilion is divided into two different circular spaces. The first symbol-

izes the indigenous house whilst the second is imaginary and is made of wooden totems with the same measurements as the Oca, to mark out this central space as suitable for rituals and festivals which will happen right in the center of the place. The form of the structure is a semi-sphere like Brazilian huts or Nordic ice houses. Both come together to create a dome on a human scale which symbolizes a meeting point: the dialogue

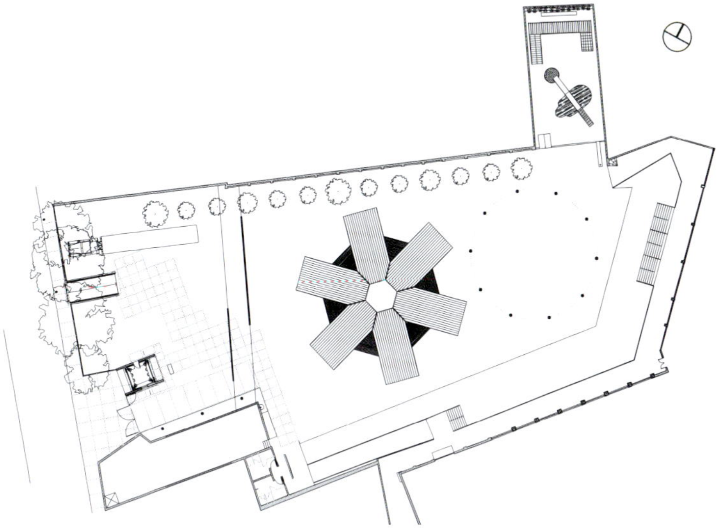

Site plan

Just like the ventilation openings of traditional igloos, the pavilion opens into the center of the space and creates the central focus for ceremonies and meetings.

Cross sections

Volumetric sketch

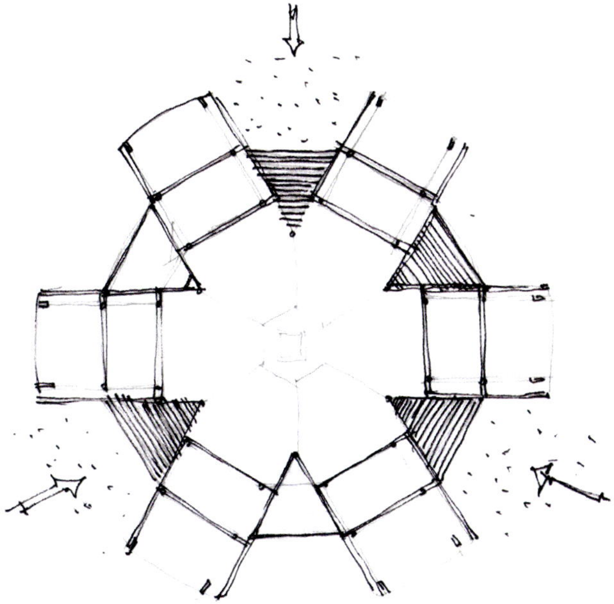

Structural plan

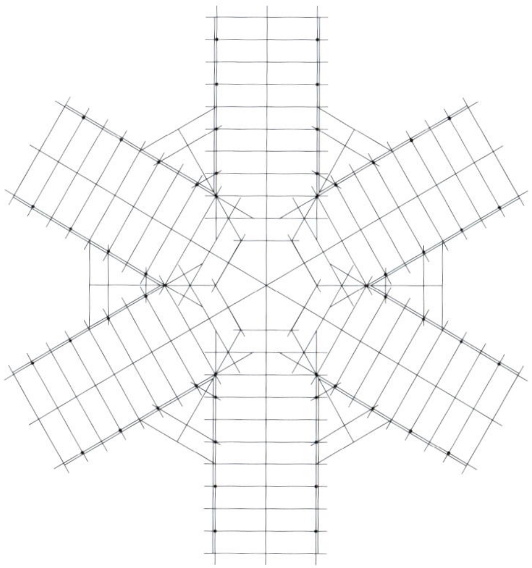

Sketch of the floor plan

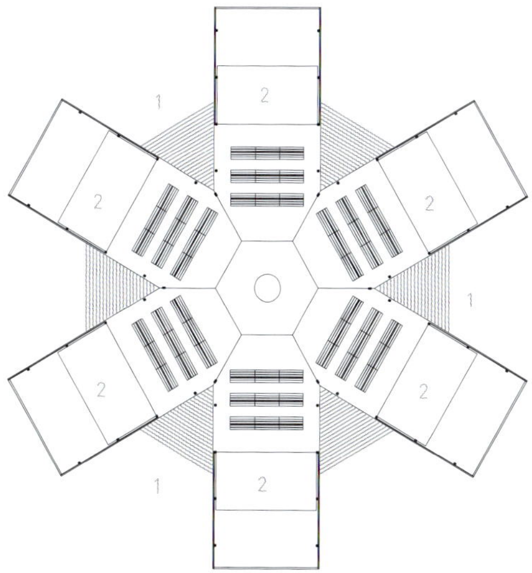

1 Entrance
2 Rooms

Plan

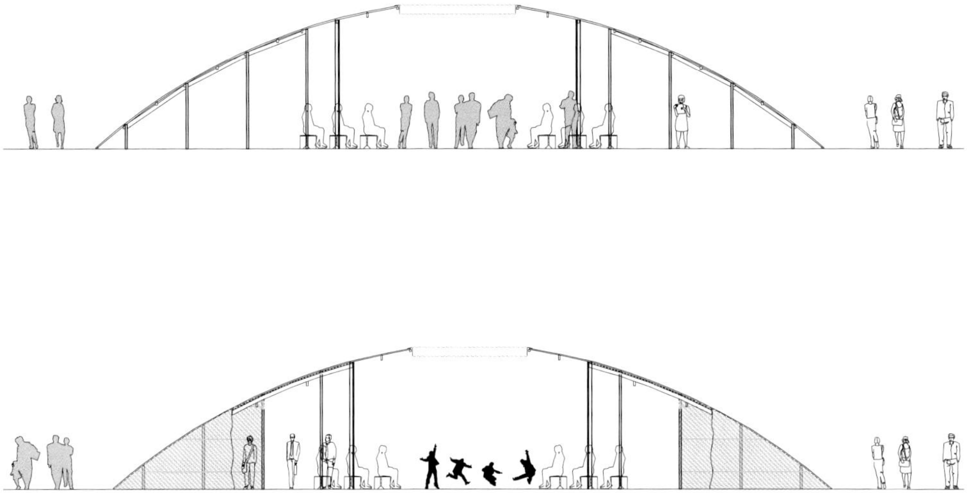

Cross sections

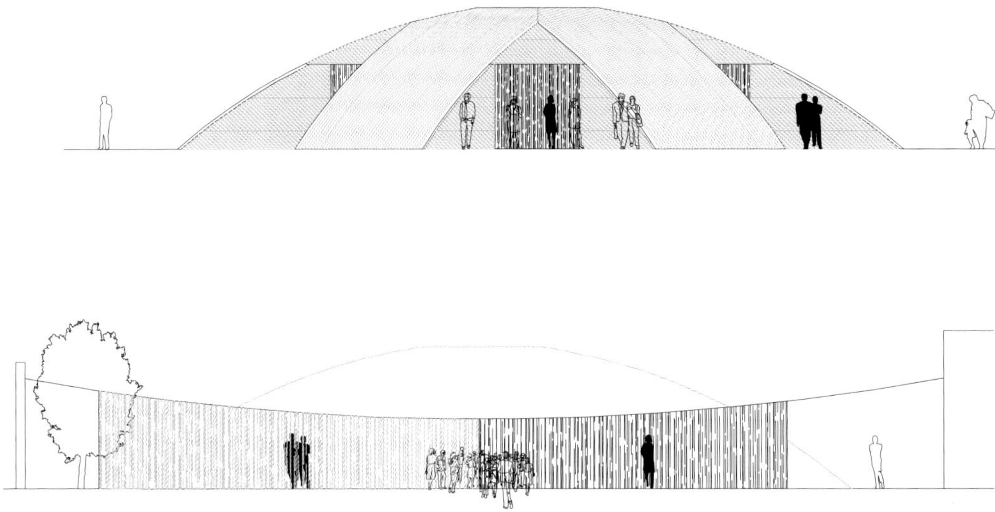

Elevations

Covering the structure with sheets of metal and wood creates a light-filled space and a subtle relationship between the interior and the exterior.

starting from elements taken from the surrounding habitat—wood and ice respectively. Complex problems have been resolved skillfully by human ingenuity and simple solutions since time immemorial, such as the choice of materials, the ventilation system, or the creation of a comfortable temperature.

The igloo represents a protective shell in a frozen environment, whilst huts are shelters from hot weather or extreme humidity. However, the principles of vernacular architecture are repeated in different geographical locations despite having to find answers to completely opposite problems.

INTERVIEW WITH **Alexandre Hepner of Königsberger Vannucchi Arquitectura**

"VERNACULAR ARCHITECTURE REPRESENTS KNOWLEDGE ACCUMULATED OVER HUNDREDS OF GENERATIONS WHICH SHOWS SIMPLE SOLUTIONS TO VERY COMPLEX PROBLEMS."

Is this project inspired by the traditional igloo?
No, not exactly by the igloo, but by another type of vernacular structure from Brazil called the oca. It is a hut built by indigenous people and, in contrast to the igloo, fulfils the function of insulating the inside from a very hot and humid climate. It has to be sufficiently open to facilitate ventilation, but at the same time it must protect the inhabitants from dangerous animals and at times from enemy tribes.

Does this analogy allow you to analyze it from another perspective?
Yes, in an unexpected way. We clearly see the relationship with the Brazilian ocas, but it is interesting that from another view it can be connected to a different typology, perhaps nearer to you. It makes us think more about the similarities which different types of vernacular architecture can be driven by totally disparate preoccupations.

What importance does vernacular architecture have in your work?
Great importance, although we recognize that it is not applied as much as it should be in our architectural environment. Brazil is a country with a very rich culture and abundant examples of vernacular architecture, too often ignored by local architects.

What can we learn from vernacular architecture and how should we apply this knowledge to contemporary architecture?
Vernacular architecture represents knowledge accumulated over hundreds of generations which shows simple solutions to very complex problems, which are difficult for one person alone to solve. That is why we believe that its importance does not stem from a simple reproduction of these structures, but from the solutions that they can offer regarding problems with materials or thermal or acoustic issues.

Why do you believe that the igloo has become an icon so closely linked to vernacular dwellings?
It is a very simple design, composed of a single material, the only one that the Inuit have at their disposal in that terrain. It represents mankind's capacity to develop ingenious, simple, and efficient solutions in the most adverse situations.

HONESTINO GUIMARÃES NATIONAL MUSEUM

ARCHITECT Oscar Niemeyer
LOCATION Brasilia, Brazil

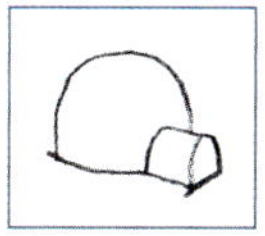

TYPE OF PROJECT Museum
AREA 156,077 ft^2 (14,500 m^2)
YEAR OF COMPLETION 2006
PHOTOS © Andrés Otero

Situated inside Brazil's largest cultural center (Cultural Complex of the Republic), is the Honestino Guimarães National Museum (Museo Nacional Honestino Guimarães). It was opened in 2006, almost fifty years late, and on the same day that the architect celebrated his ninety-ninth birthday. Oscar Niemeyer was given the task of completing this ambitious project which gave a city like Brasilia the artistic facilities of a capital city.

Undoubtedly, the building of the National Museum is the icon of the Cultural Complex situated in the Esplanade of the Ministries. Just 295 ft (90 m) in diameter, it forms a great dome over the garden area. The initial project contained two asymmetrical openings in the upper part of the building, providing the necessary light for the garden with a panoramic restaurant on the top floor. But whilst it was being built, these were eliminated to make space for a simple

dome with a sloped ramp for access: a clean and serene shape, 92 ft (28 m) high. The building is visually connected to the library behind it. In this project, Niemeyer, above all, valued simplicity—simple and austere lines in harmony with the surroundings are characteristics that are also appreciated in the vernacular dwellings of the Inuit. The semicircular form has an interior which is vaulted and accommodating, capable of showing off the artists who exhibit in this space.

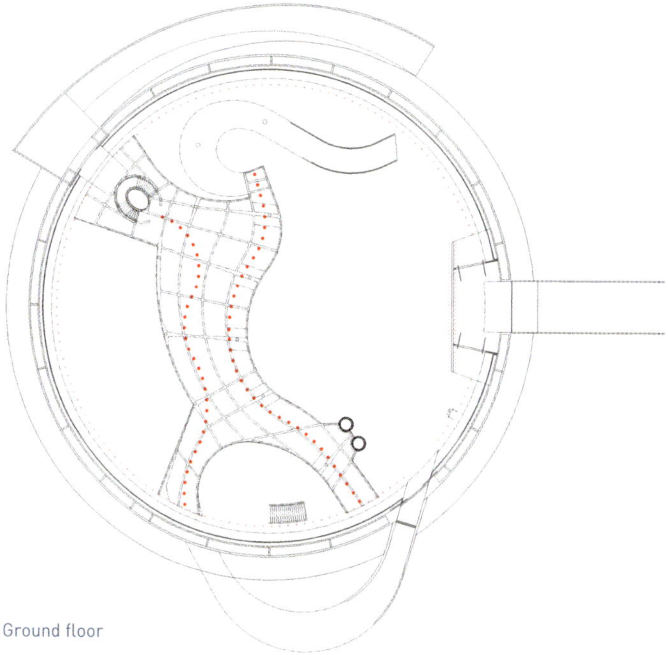

Ground floor

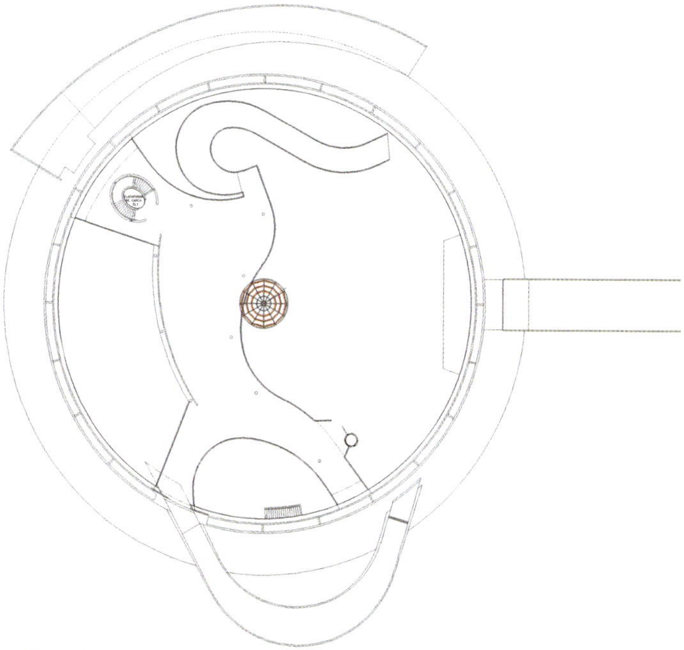

Mezzanine

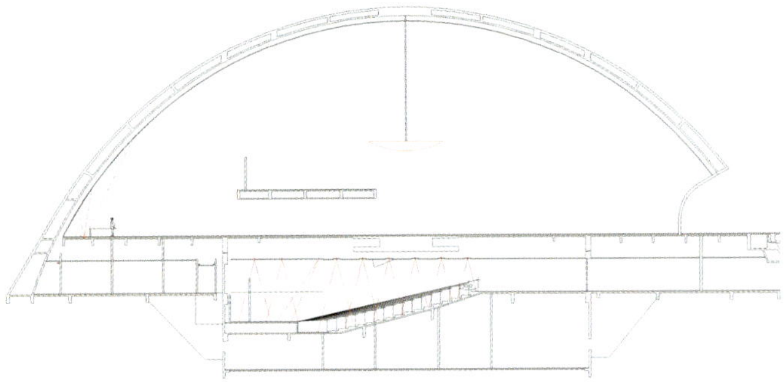

Cross section

A structure on a human level with the maximum volume possible in the minimum surface area.

The National Museum is a construction without angles organized around a single space. The free and sensual curves made of concrete rise in architectural forms with a formal richness that comes close to the beauty of sculpture.

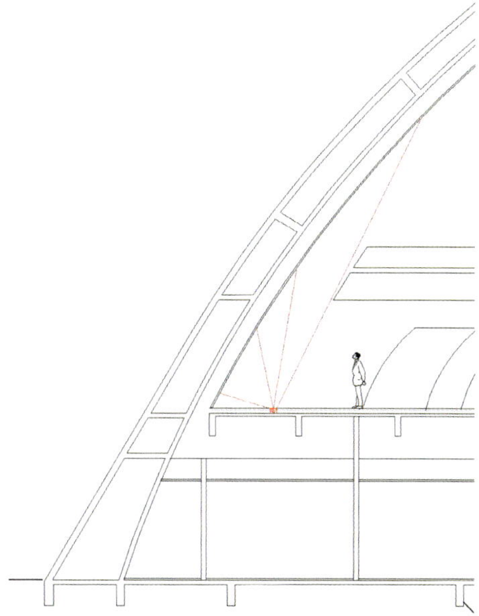

Detail of cross section

LANGUAGES PAVILLION

ARCHITECT Veech Media Architecture
LOCATION Viena, Austria

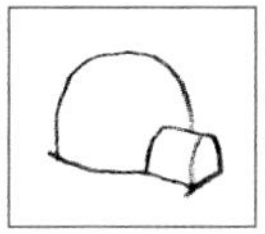

TYPE OF PROJECT Pavilion
AREA 840 ft^2 (78 m^2)
HEIGHT 16 ft (5 m)
DURATION OF CONSTRUCTION 3 months
YEAR OF COMPLETION 2001
PHOTOS © Sabine Gruber

As if it were an igloo of the future, Veech Media Architecture (VMA) opened the Languages Pavilion (May 9, 2001) at the Stephansplatz de Vienna. The project was commissioned by the Austrian Ministry of Education and Art. After opening the pavilion was sent to Austria's nine provincial capitals to celebrate the European Year of Language.

VMA admits to having a fondness for archaic building methods such as traditional igloos. From this observation came the creation of this modular installation which offers a response to the needs of new nomads in an information-focused society. The aim of the installation is to give information about the variety and importance of all the European languages, framed in the borderless new Europe. To do this, the VMA architects created a semi-sphere dome with spines covered by a PVC membrane. The protuberances with craters invite curious spectators to look through them and at the same time provide the pavilion

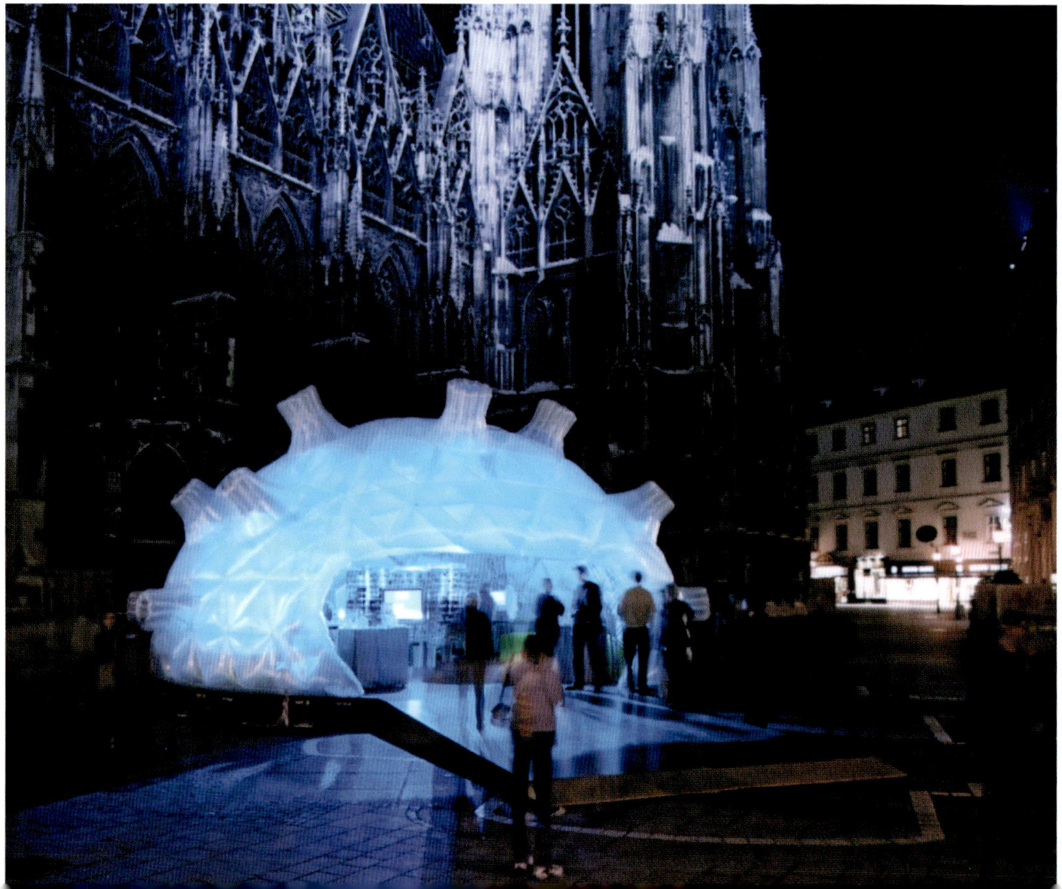

with light—an enveloping design, almost obsessive, that entices people to come close to it. It is a poetic metaphor for space, like a seed or a cell seen through the lens of a powerful microscope. Its ethereal appearance suggests more that it is a forum for debate than an information center. The human scale of the interior turns it into an environment suitable for meditation and reflection.

The PVC membrane which envelops the pavilion creates the same translucent effect as a traditional igloo.

The characteristic protuberances of this piece are small windows that invite the visitor to dive into the interior.

Sketch

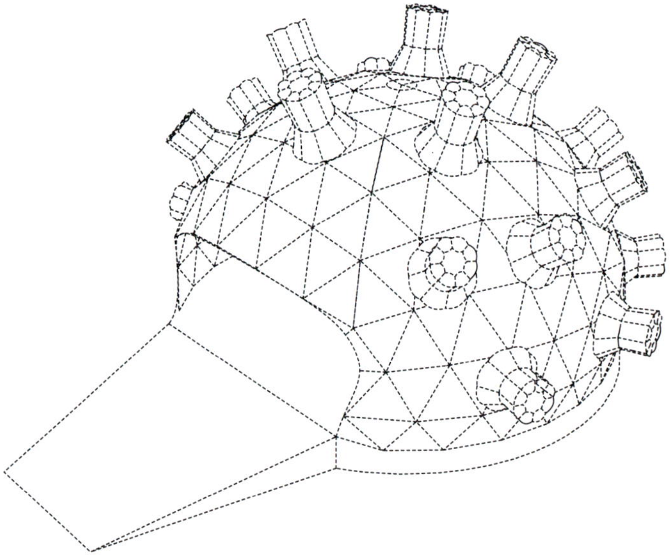

Axonometric view

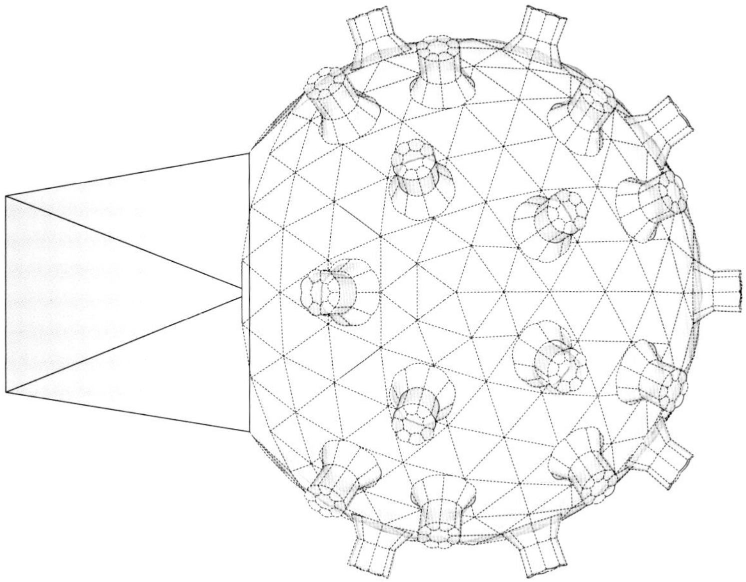

Roof plan

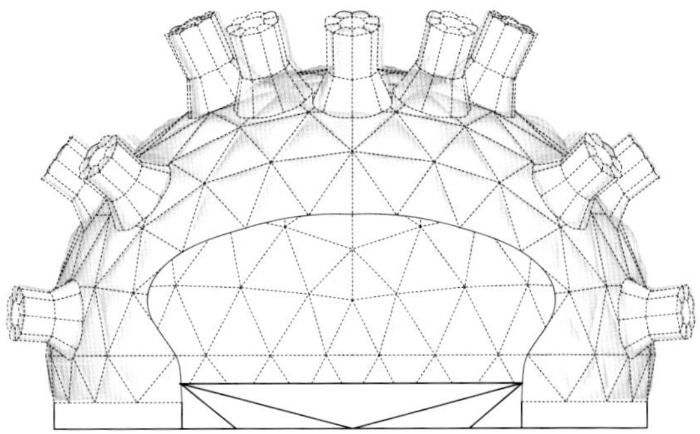

Front elevation

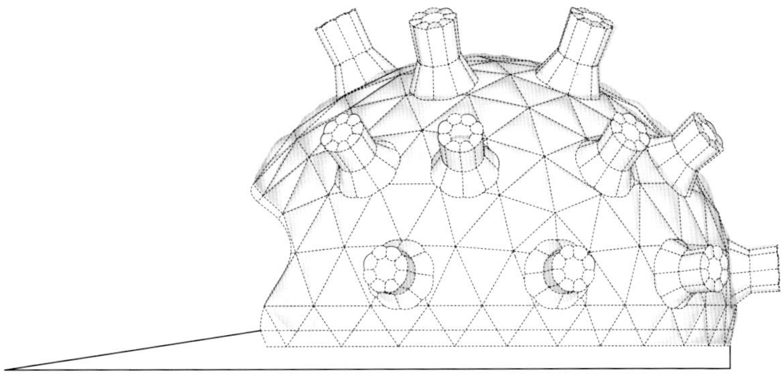

Side elevation

The pavilion is erected as a temporary intervention in the urban environment, giving a new value to the obsessive utopian designs of the 60s and 70s. VMA achieves a living architectural model, capable of being installed anywhere thanks to a simple assembly system. Here is an example of an organic structure that extols the advantages of buildings which are plain, simple, and not ostentatious and concerned only with the usefulness of the structure.

> WE MUST EXPLORE WAYS OF INCORPORATING OR FUSING THE KNOWLEDGE OF VERNACULAR ARCHITECTURE WITH TODAY'S TECHNOLOGY, BEFORE IT IS LOST FOREVER.

Do igloos and the Languages Pavilion have anything in common?

The Languages Pavilion was part of an investigation into inflatable and mobile forms, which started in 1999. There are obvious analogies between this pneumatic structure and the igloo, although in terms of material, weight, mobility, and climatic questions, they are quite different. The project has driven us to center our efforts on the examination of new materials for the next series of pneumatic structures.

What do you think, then, about this analogy?

I think that the analogy is somewhat distant; generally they are similar in terms of their luminous shape in the landscape. Their different materials, structures, and cultures obviously mean there is not a direct relationship. More than finding solutions, we ask questions and look for possibilities. For us "form follows material" and the external factors are those which give the space form. We tackle a design like an evolutionary process indirectly influenced by other disciplines, cultures, and methods.

What importance does vernacular architecture have in your work?

In the office there is cultural mix; my partner was born in Moscow and I come from Chicago, the studio is in Vienna and soon we will be opening others in London and Moscow. This mix makes us much more open. At the moment we are working in ten European cities on completely different projects. For us it is more important to add new elements to the existing context to enhance the urban landscape; that is, diversity over homogeny.

What can we learn from vernacular architecture?

Obviously there is a lot to learn from traditional types that can generate new directions in contemporary architecture. It depends a lot on the research and the methods used in reinterpreting the information and producing something new. Traditional building techniques are being replaced or systematically eradicated by digital production and manufacturing. We must explore ways of incorporating or fusing the knowledge of vernacular architecture with today's technology, before it is lost forever. Our profession is one that needs more human interaction and fewer boundaries to achieve advanced results. Who knows if we might design an igloo one day, in the future...

Why do you believe that the igloo has become an icon so closely linked to vernacular dwellings?

On the one hand, the igloo is a traditional structure restricted to a very specific part of the planet. On the other, there is the romantic image of the solitary igloo on the frozen landscape, lit by the hearth inside which gives heat to its inhabitants whilst they tell stories and the family eats together. It is here that the essence of architecture—that of providing shelter—becomes something deeper, a creation of a meeting place for exchanging experiences, views, and opinions. The contrast of the severity of the extreme conditions of the Arctic with the human warmth inside the igloo creates an image that is stamped on our collective imagination.

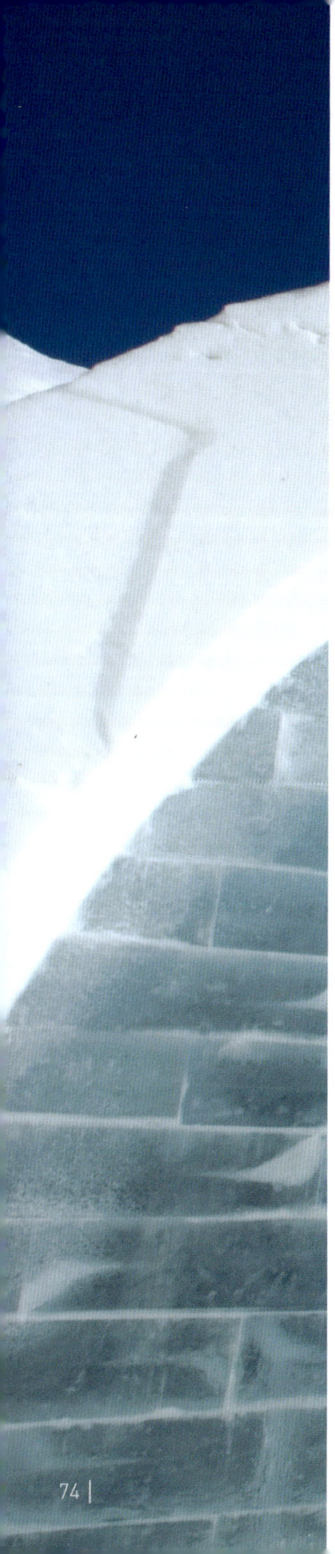

HÔTEL DE GLACE

ARCHITECT Brière, Gilbert + associés (architects) and Serge Péloquin (artistic director)
LOCATION Quebec, Canada

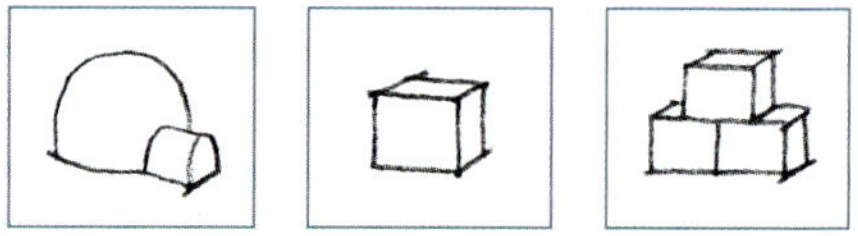

TYPE OF PROJECT Hotel
AREA 32,292 ft^2 (3,000 m^2)
HEIGHT 21 ft (6.5 m)
DURATION OF CONSTRUCTION 6 to 7 months
YEAR OF COMPLETION 2001, first version (rebuilt every year)
PHOTOS © Xavier Dachez
© Serge Péloquin

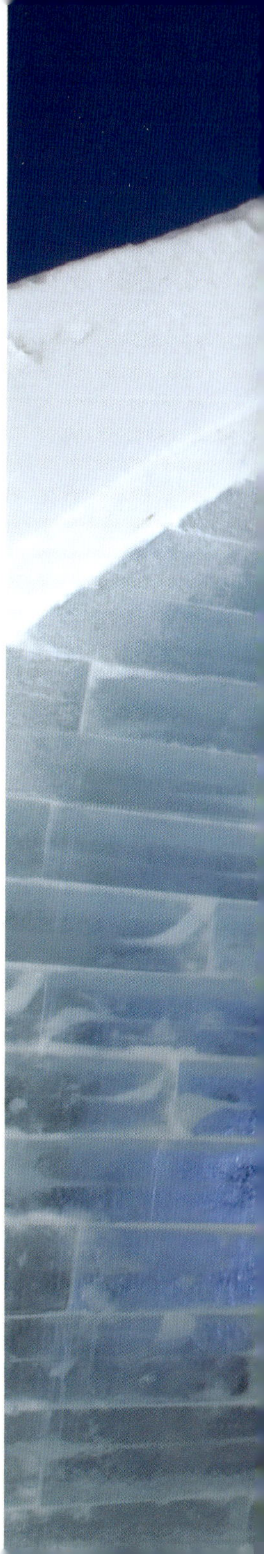

With an area of 32,292 ft^2 (3,000 m^2) roofs reaching 21 ft (6 m) in height, the impressive ice hotel in Québec is built in the majestic atmosphere of Sainte-Catherine-de-la-Jacques-Cartier. To fit out the 36 rooms and suites available, 15,000 tons of snow and 500 of ice were needed.

Directed by Serge Péloquin, this monumental artistic work with a temporary lifespan opens its doors in January and disappears little by little in the middle of April. The ice melts and the water returns to the river to bring other places to life. It is not built of blocks of ice, but is made of a series of snow arches. Artificial snow is wetter than natural snow and can be molded more easily. Once hardened by the ice, it gives the vault more stability.

The structure is supported by the installation of formwork built from two sheets of stainless steel that meet at the top of a Gothic arch. Snow houses are well developed constructions that do

not alter the ecosystem in any way. The Hôtel de Glace is directly inspired by the building techniques of the first communities in the area and the creators of this ambitious project wanted to respect the aesthetics of the igloo. Péloquin continues to use snow as a raw material, although to work with it, he avails himself of modern technology. This expression of architecture aims to be an educational, recreational, and creative experience that wakes up visitors' sensibilities in an environ-

The colors show the different phases of the hotel's construction.

Plan for casts

Plan for formwork

1 Main entrance
2 Lobby
3 Slide
4 Bar
5 Club
6 Rooms
7 Spa
8 Chapel

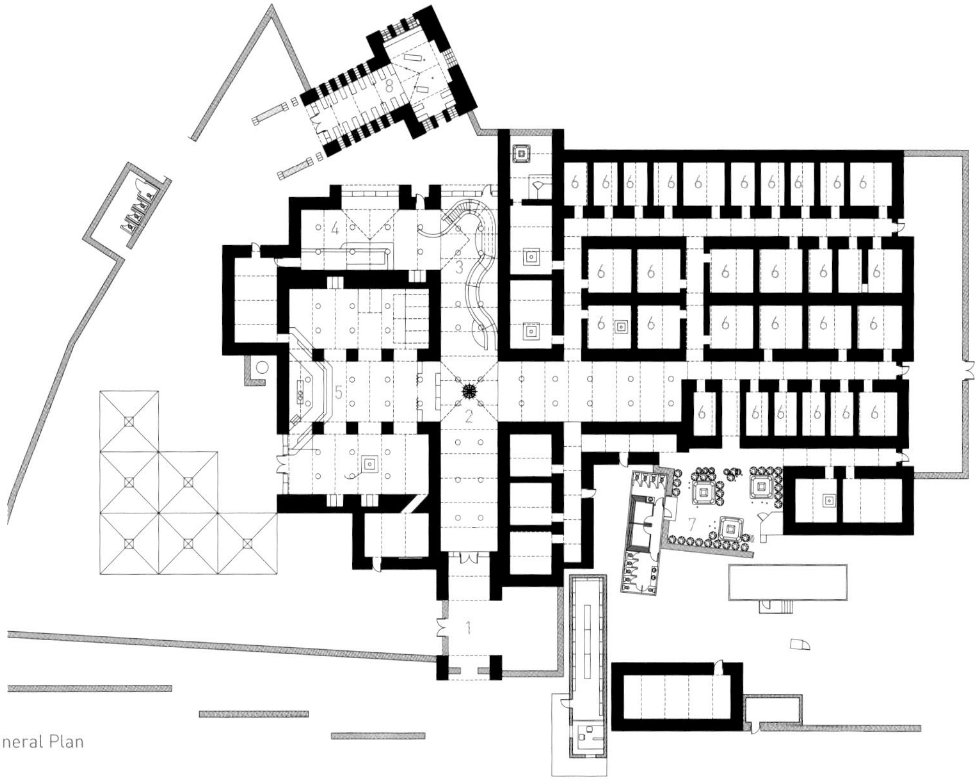

General Plan

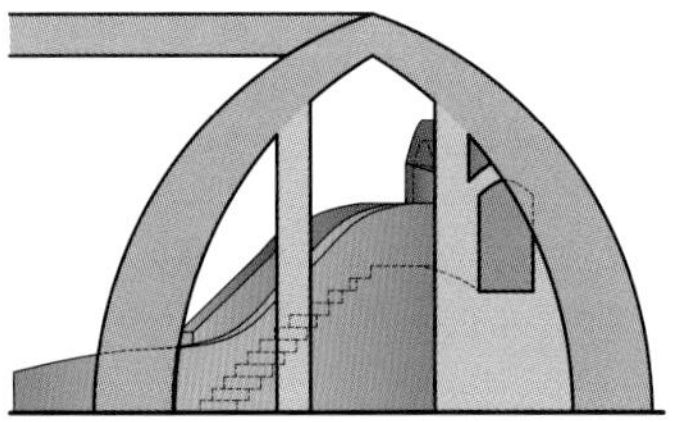

Transverse cross section of slide

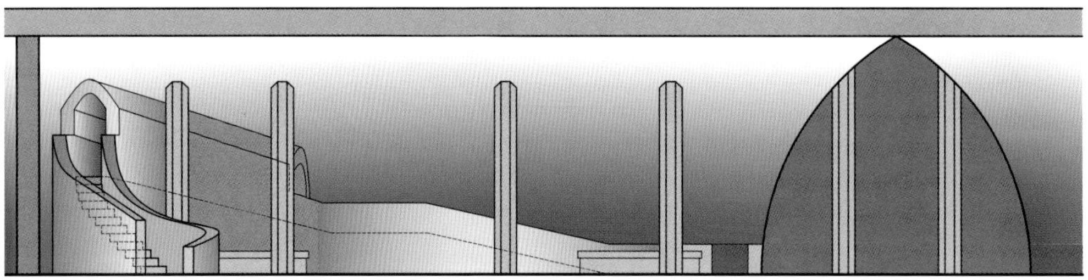

Longitudinal cross section of slide

mental context in which nature is shown in its purest state. This is an opportunity for modern man to revive the culture of ancient Canadian nomadic society by looking at their vernacular buildings, which are capable of transmitting their social and spiritual values.

Compacted snow is used for the general structure, ice for the translucent openings, and wood for the entrances and exits.

The hotel establishes a strong link with the ancestral traditions of the region.

INTERVIEW WITH **SERGE PÉLOQUIN**

> THE FORM A BUILDING TAKES IS OFTEN A METAPHOR FOR THE COSMOS...ASSOCIATED WITH POWERFUL SPIRITUAL VALUES THAT ALLOW A PEOPLE'S CULTURAL IDENTITY TO BE DEFINED FOR CENTURIES.

In what way did the context influence the design of the Hôtel de Glace?

Canada is composed of five large cultural regions defined by their climatic, geographical, and ecological characteristics. Each region has given rise to different architectural forms which reflect these characteristics as well as the available building materials, lifestyles, and the social and spiritual values of the inhabitants of each place. The Hôtel de Glace is directly inspired by the building techniques of the First Nations, techniques that we have reproduced by using modern adapted technology, using snow and ice as raw materials.

How important is the observation of vernacular architecture in your work?

Vernacular architecture is synonymous with indigenous and domestic architecture, from a place indifferent to strange or foreign influences. Our architecture of snow and ice does not only fulfill the function of giving shelter to its visitors, but also expresses in a comprehensive fashion the techniques and qualities of buildings in northern cultures.

What did you want to contribute with this reference to vernacular buildings and the igloo in particular?

The Hôtel de Glace is an ephemeral construction which lasts for three months. When spring arrives, it melts and returns to the river to create life once again in another place. We are very respectful of the purity and the aesthetics of the context. We follow all the construction regulations, for example in terms of the emergency exits and their lighting, the size of the doors, the electricity supply under the snow etc., to achieve this version of the northern phenomenon. The hotel is an educational, recreational, and creative experience that wakes up visitors' sensibilities to surroundings in which nature forms a vital part of society.

Man constructs and makes use of his surroundings at the same time. His technical skills depend on three interactive environments: human, natural, and material. The igloo is the mark of a very special community that still hides many mysteries.

Why do you think that the igloo has become such a cherished icon of the home?

Buildings play two clear roles; they are used as a shelter and they become a tangible link with the universe. The form a building takes is often a metaphor for the cosmos, and as such, is associated with powerful spiritual values that allow a people's cultural identity to be defined for centuries. The actual word "igloo" evokes a frequently misunderstood world: the life of the Inuit and the unique spirit of the polar universe.

FORESTRY DEPARTMENT OF WALLONIA

ARCHITECT Philippe SAMYN and PARTNERS

LOCATION Marche-en-Famenne, Belgium

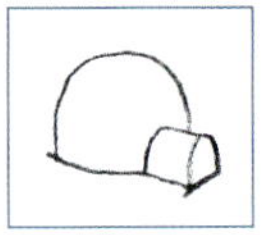

TYPE OF PROJECT Forestry Department office

AREA 12,325 ft^2 (1,145 m^2)

HEIGHT 42 ft (12.7 m)

DURATION OF CONSTRUCTION 3 years

YEAR OF COMPLETION 1995

PHOTOS © Ch.Bastin and J.Evrard, Daylight Liège sprl, Philippe SAMYN and PARTNERS, M-Fr Plissart.

Created by Philippe SAMYN and PARTNERS in 2004, this forestry conservation center is situated right in the heart of the Ardennes Forest, in the Wallonian part of Belgium. Inside there is a laboratory for cultivating seeds from the region's mountains.

The structure that covers the whole building consists of wooden arches held in place by concrete bases. The semi-circle is covered by 1,700 tiles made of laminated reflective glass that, even in adverse weather, allow for maximum advantage to be taken of the sunlight. It is a type of building adapted to the environmental conditions as much in its design as in the use of its materials and energy in terms of sustainability. A basic element of the structure is the double arched layer made of new wood, which better resists the tension it is under from the curvature. Inside the shell there are two secondary buildings, placed lengthways on both sides, which house the offices, the store

The small pieces of glass adapt to the cylindrical form of the building thanks to the modeling of the wooden structure supporting them.

rooms, and the small laboratories. The central section is reserved for the machinery that treats and dries the seeds. The dome imitates the organic form of the northern igloos, creating a place adapted to humans, similar to a womb, framed by idyllic surroundings for studying the art of forest conservation.

Creating a space for forestry in the middle of such a valuable natural location requires a high level of mimesis with the context. It is essential

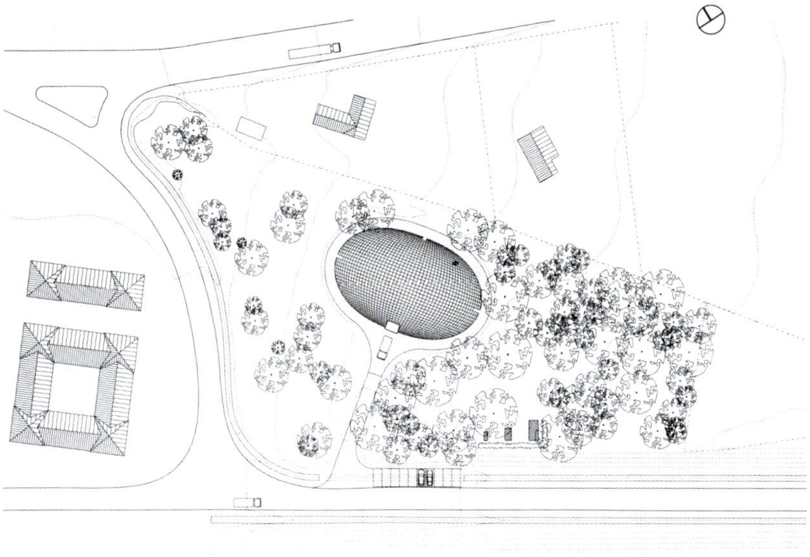

Site plan

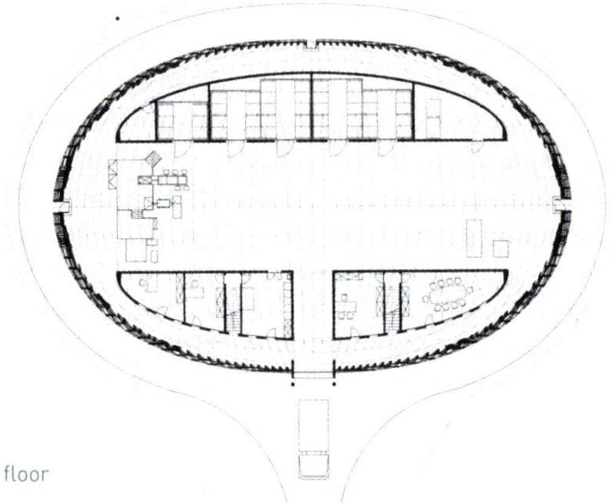

Ground floor

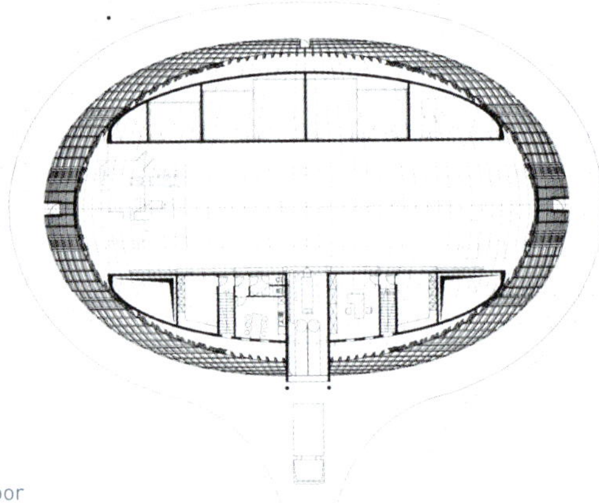

First floor

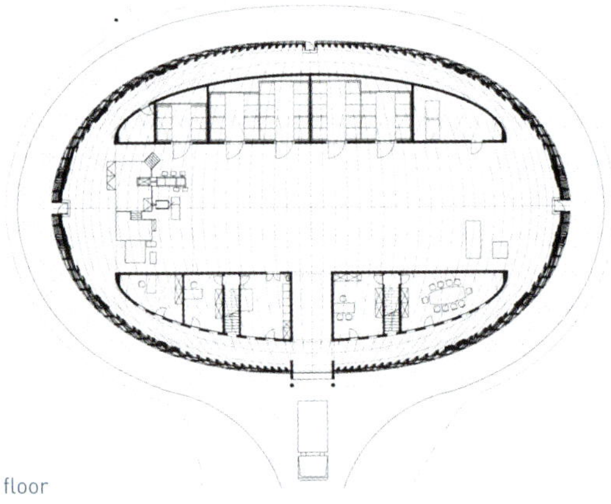

Second floor

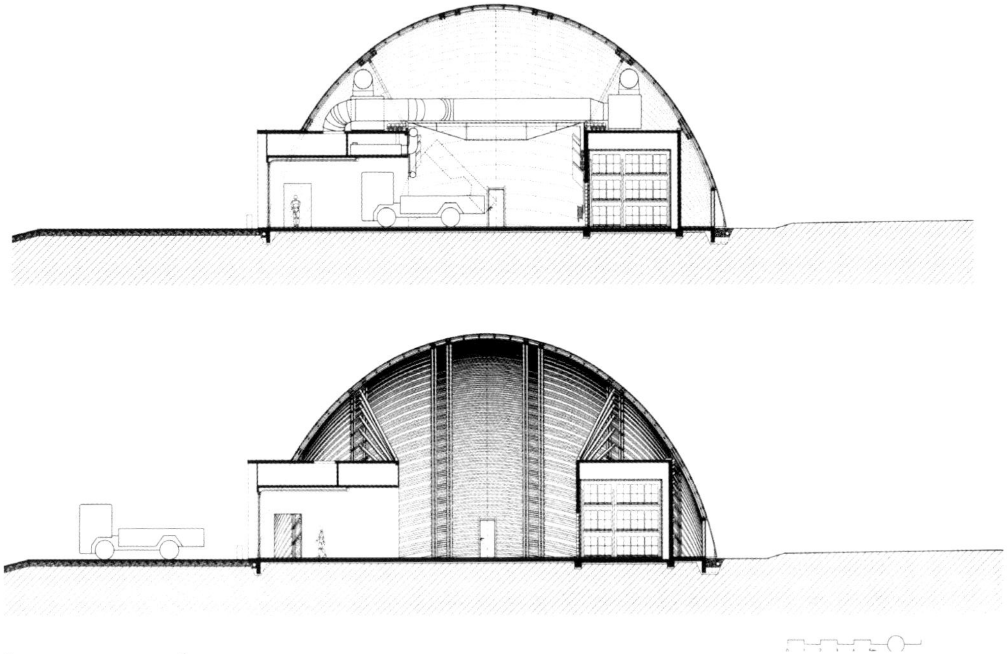

Transverse cross sections

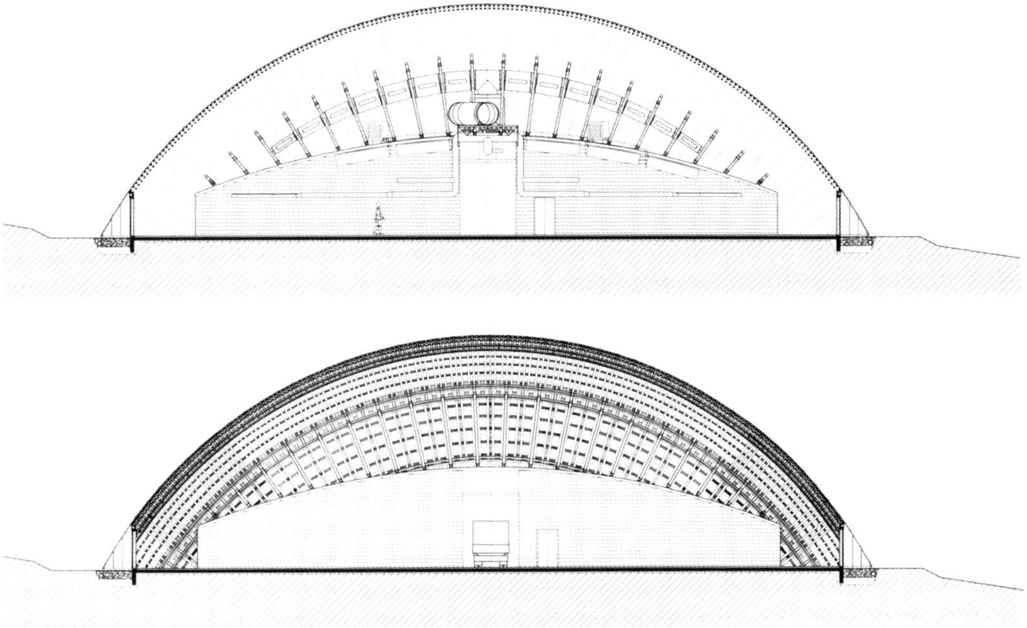

Longitudinal cross sections

not to interfere more than necessary in the habitat where the building is to be built. This representation of the design of the austere ice house manages to dissolve into the actual ecosystem, profiting from it as much as possible by using the latest technical advances: a modern human shelter right in the middle of nature.

The simple materials and the visible installations show the premise of creating a highly efficient building with minimum resources.

PREFAB MODULE FOR ANTARCTICA

ARCHITECT Marko Matulic Cvitanic

LOCATION Glaciar Collins, Isla Rey Jorge, Península Antártica Chilena

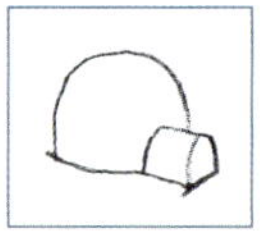 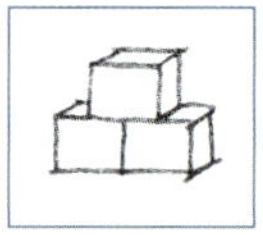

TYPE OF PROJECT Prefabricated module

AREA 172 ft^2 (16 m^2)

HEIGHT 13 ft (4 m)

DURATION OF CONSTRUCTION 30 months

YEAR OF COMPLETION 2006

PHOTOS © Marko Matulic Cvitanic

The architect Marko Matulic Cvitanic explored a new building system to create a sleeping module that can house two people in extreme conditions. With the backing of the Chilean Antarctica Institute, he created a proposal for something that would meet the structural and environmental requirements of areas like Antarctica, was easy to transport, and fast and efficient to assemble.

The module reinterprets the architectural paradigm of the igloo with a prefabricated system of self standing arches which are both structure and insulation; they are designed to achieve different configurations of space. The set of arches are made from a series of pieces of expanded polystyrene, which are like the ice blocks of the traditional igloo. All these blocks fit together and are tightened by steel cables to achieve a resis-

tant and autonomous structure, where the pieces of polystyrene take the force of compression and the steel cables the traction. This makes a minimum prototype: a sleeping space of 172 ft^2 (16 m^2) suitable for housing two people. A series of six arches made of fourteen blocks of polystyrene make up a united structural shell which resists the weather and the snow. This shell is anchored to the ground structure by a platform of six adjustable legs. A covering made from high resistance, orange PVC fabric makes the whole structure waterproof and allows it to heat up easily.

In this project, the study of vernacular architecture provides fundamental principles for the structure as well as the insulation or assembly. Matulic has found a form on a human scale that can be made easily by its users, and at

The structural model: the vault of tightened blocks makes up part of a system to which other units can be added.

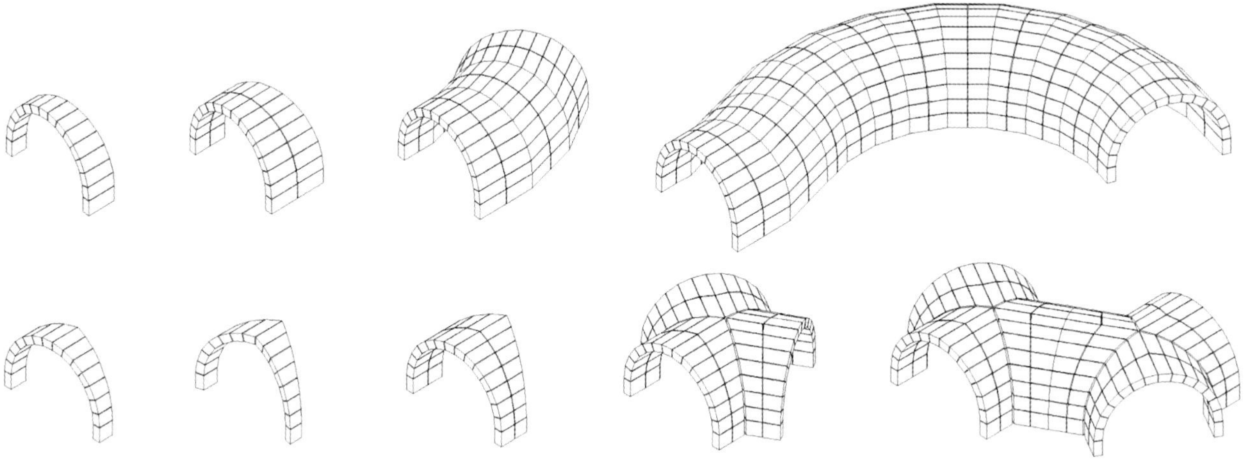

Studies of the fit between modules

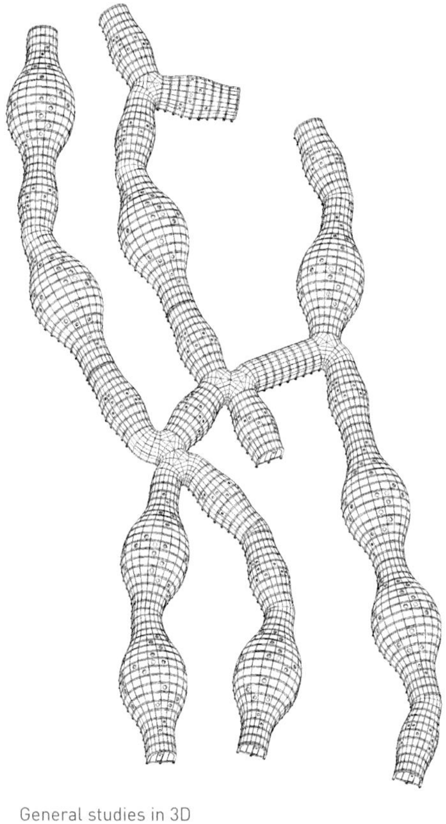

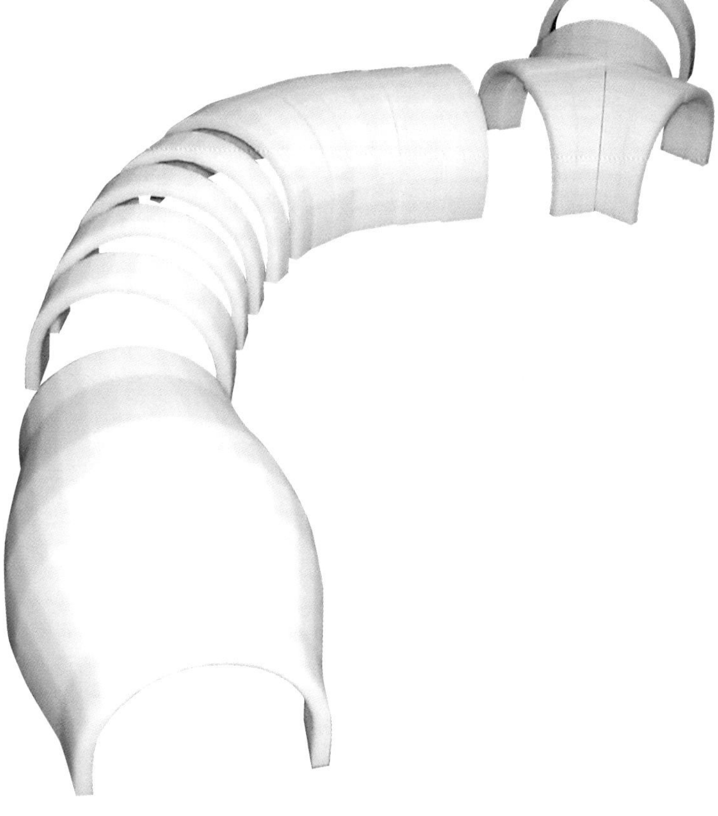

General studies in 3D

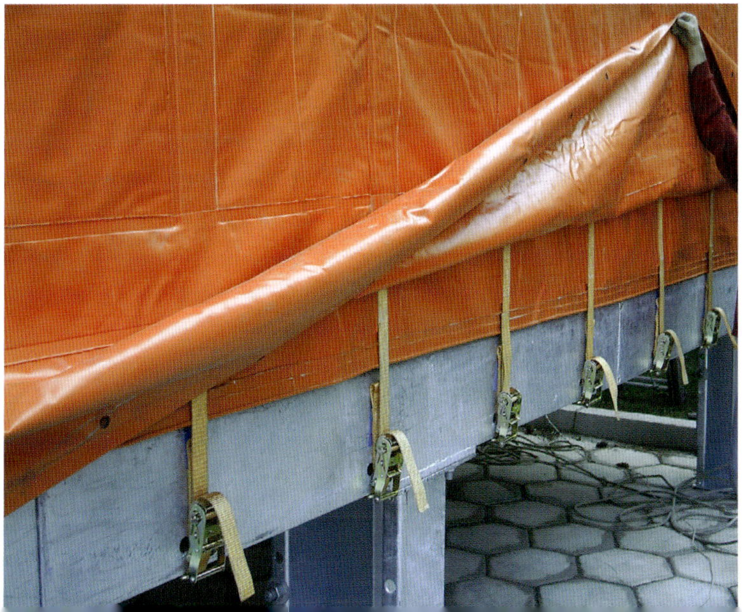

The construction system of this module, entirely prefabricated and removable, allows it to be installed easily anywhere.

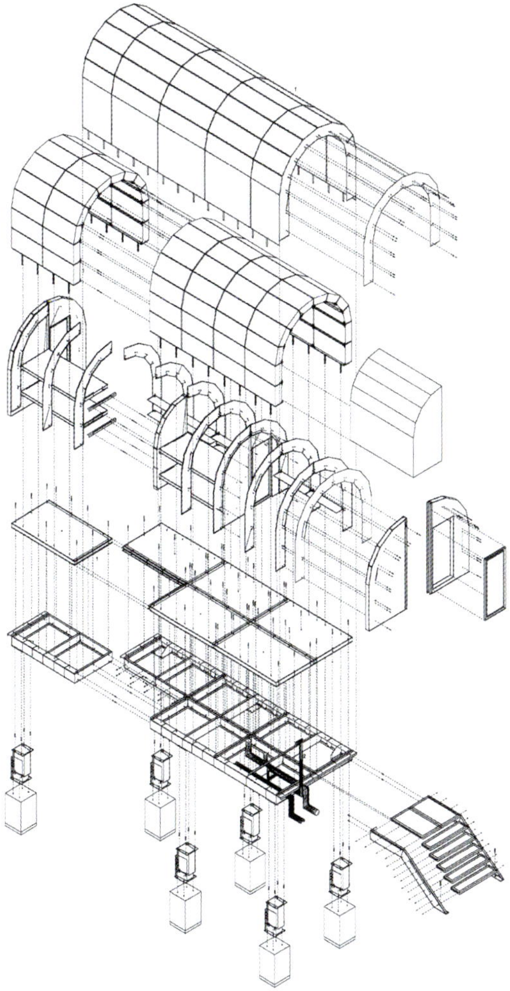

the same time provides maximum comfort. This effort reconsiders concepts that are hundreds of years old in the same context in order to create a new igloo that uses all the advantages of today's advances.

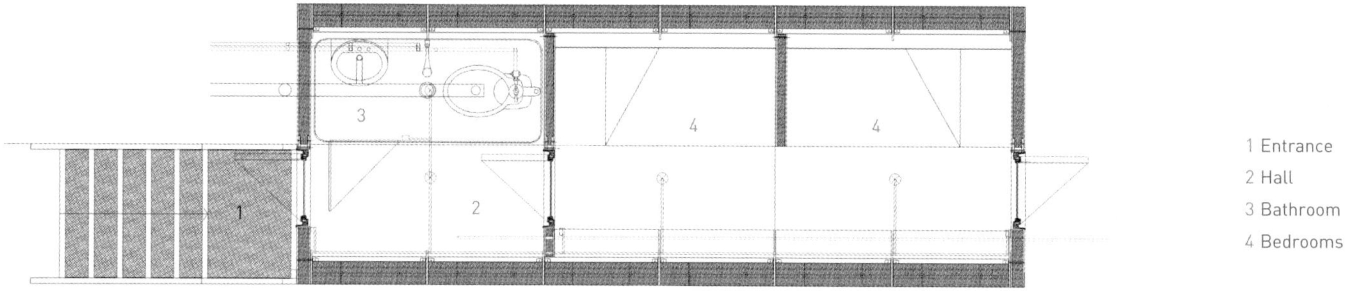

Floor plan

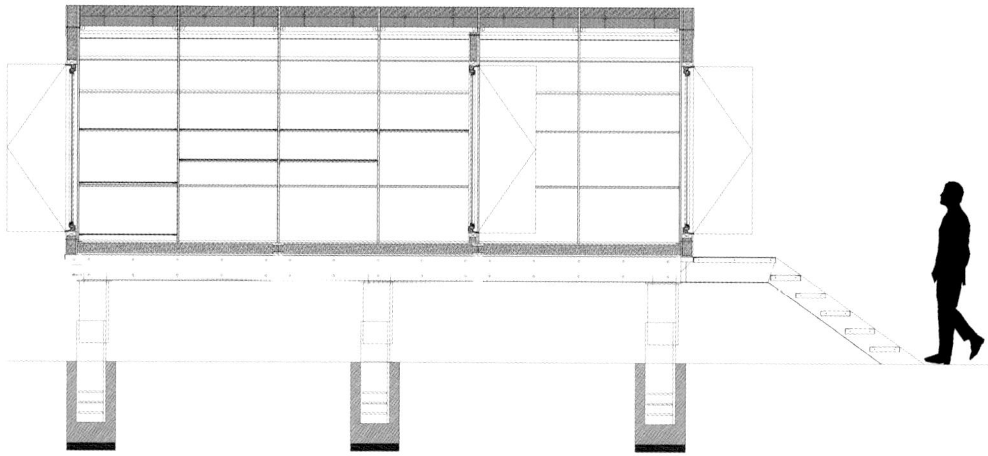

Longitudinal cross section

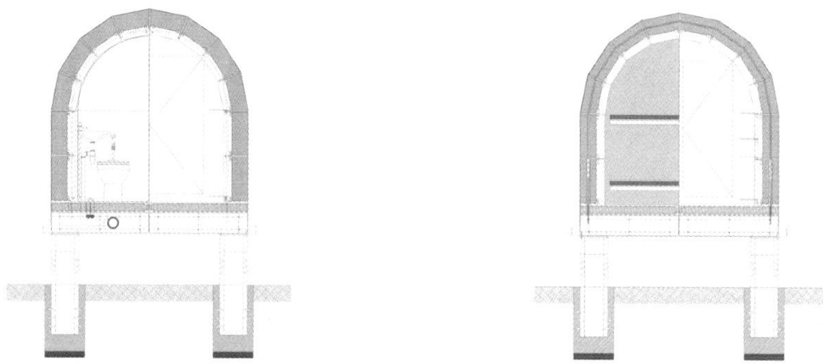

Transverse cross section

INTERVIEW WITH MARKO MATULIC CVITANIC

> THE PRINCIPLES OF VERNACULAR ARCHITECTURE SHOULD BE REINTERPRETED TOGETHER WITH THE TECHNOLOGICAL DEVELOPMENT OF OUR GENERATION AND THE CULTURE OF OUR PEOPLE.

What relationship does your project have with the traditional igloo?

The project is based on the main design characteristics of the igloo. The living space was reduced to a minimum to facilitate the heating of the interior, a shell was created composed of self supporting arches resistant to snow falls and strong winds, and the same system of crossing ventilation was incorporated to optimize energy efficiency. The concept of insulation has also been reinterpreted through a thick thermal mass, and the assembly process based on simple, repeatable individual pieces that two or three people, the actual users, can put together easily.

What importance does vernacular architecture have in your work?

It is fundamental, and especially in this case. Essentially, vernacular architecture offers an enormous amount of information about the design and contraction in a particular context, knowledge that has been developed and tested through the experience of many generations.

What can we learn from vernacular architecture and how can this knowledge be applied to contemporary architecture?

I think that the most important lessons are related to its close relationship to the climate, the culture, and the people of a particular area. In this sense, these principles should be reinterpreted together with the technological development of our generation and the culture of our people. By this I mean that these principles are basically the same today as they were hundreds of years ago; what we need to do is incorporate them and at the same time take advantage of new materials, the design tools, and the new forms of energy, amongst other things..

Why do you believe that the igloo has become an icon so closely linked to vernacular dwellings?

I think that the igloo has been a paradigm for the development of a building in cold climates; it is a concept that efficiently resolves the most significant problems these conditions bring. It is an excellent synthesis of form and construction that responds to the conditions of the climate and the location, which are characteristic of these extreme areas.

attendants office
childrens toilets

DIANA, PRINCESS OF WALES MEMORIAL PLAYGROUND

ARCHITECT Jestico+Whiles
LOCATION London, United Kingdom

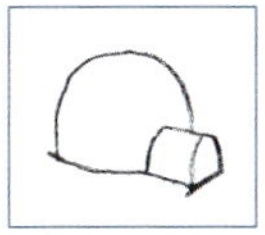

TYPE OF PROJECT Equipment
AREA 1,184 ft^2 (110 m^2)
HEIGHT 16 ft (5 m)
DURATION OF CONSTRUCTION 6 months
YEAR OF COMPLETION 2002
PHOTOS © James Morris

The majestic Kensington Gardens in London house this imaginative corner in memory of the English "Queen of Hearts." This is a final tribute to the Princess of Wales and a reflection of her interest in children and the family. Jestico+Whiles have created a space designed for the children to play in inspired by the home of J. M. Barrie's famous creation, Peter Pan.

Hidden underneath a mound of earth is a vaulted structure covered by a fresh blanket of glass. It is a home under the ground, rough and simple, that offers a welcoming and familiar shelter. The design was carefully modeled by computer, adjusting it to the height of children and adults. The openings in the upper part of the construction bring to mind the round holes which allow ventilation in igloos. These three cones are strategically positioned to provide light to the interior spaces. The dome generates a playful and private interior and an exterior that blends in with the

surrounding landscape. The chameleon-like nature of this space, able to adapt to the environment, calls to mind the idea of a hiding place, or protection, just like the igloo was for members of the Inuit community. The figures of the children from Never Never Land, which throw intriguing shadows in the room, are found etched on the outer doors—a home in which a modern-day Peter and Wendy can reinterpret their numerous adventures of the eternal child.

1 Entrance
2 Office
3 First aid
4 Bathroom
5 Service access

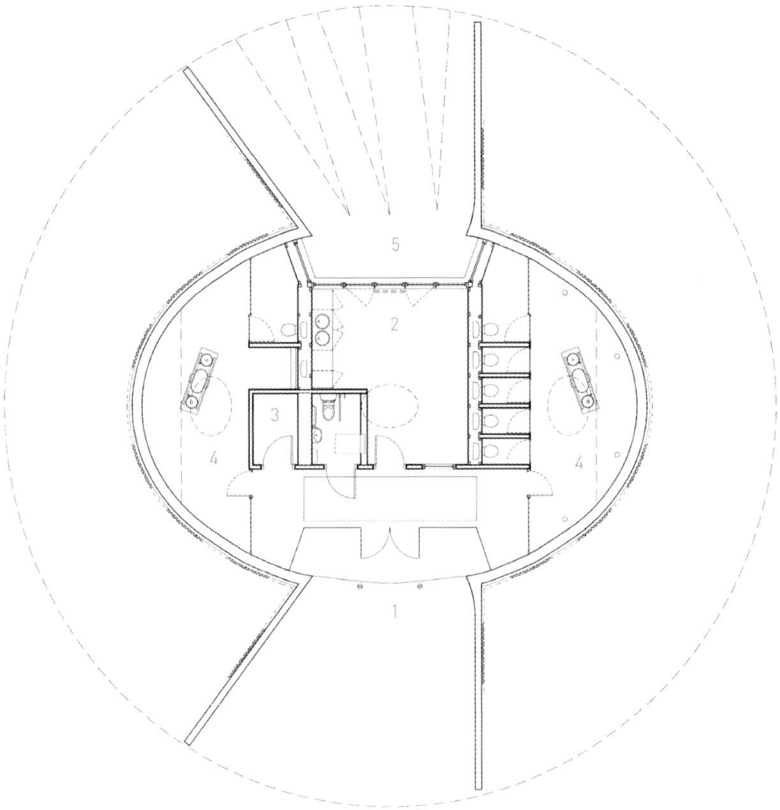

Floor plan

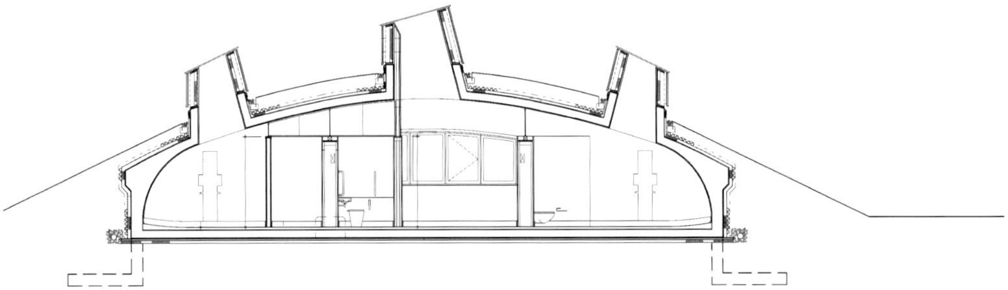

Longitudinal cross section

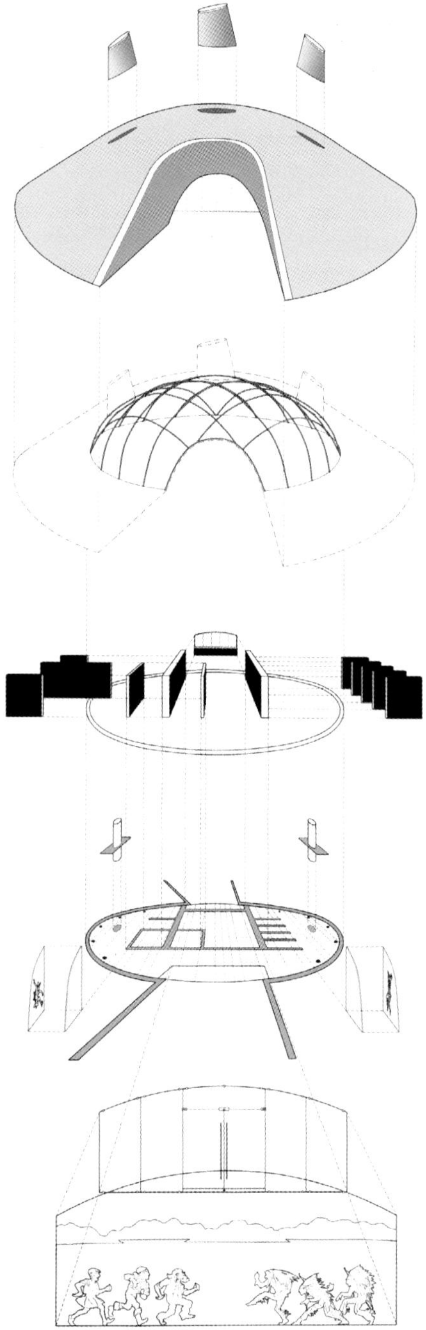

Exploded view

Like a modern igloo adapted to the mild climate, the ice is replaced by earth, grass, cement, and glass, applying new technologies to build the project. The semi-sphere shape is a universally repeated structure that bears the earliest symbol of wellbeing: the maternal belly of Mother Nature, manifested in a fusion between the playing area and the hill that it rises from.

UKENDT

ARCHITECT Anja Franke (artist) and John Southern (architect)
LOCATION Los Angeles, California, United States

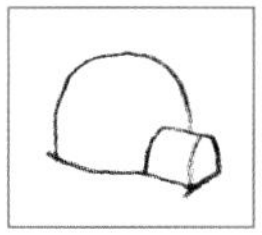

TYPE OF PROJECT Installation
SURFACE 301 ft^2 (28 m^2)
HEIGHT 10 ft (3 m)
DURATION OF CONSTRUCTION 6 weeks
YEAR OF COMPLETION 2007
PHOTOS © John Southern, Polly Crongeyer, Materials & Applications

This Nordic-inspired installation, erected on a patio on Silver Lake Boulevard in Los Angeles, fuses the vernacular construction of Eskimo societies with the native materials of the Californian climate. This original project, which juxtaposes conflicting elements in the same piece, was born from a collaboration between Danish artist Anja Franke and North American architect John Southern.

The structure of an igloo is a starting point, the use of organic materials like bamboo or rattan, together with others of industrial origin (such as the felt that covers the whole surface of the dome with interconnected sheets), shows the eclectic nature of the construction. The application of these materials and structures was facilitated by Nicholas Blake and the team at the Architecture Experimental M&A (Materials & Applications) gallery.

For three years they joined forces with the architects of the project for some intense work.

Type of Californian bamboo used in the construction of the Igloo/Ukendt

In a contemporary context like Los Angeles, the artistic installation of Franke and Southern goes back to the intrinsic values of the traditional igloo, such as human warmth, the family unit, and a base for survival in a hostile external environment. Far from trying to create a new architectural archetype for the twenty-first century, the creators use the Igloo/Ukendt to show the relevance of cultural exchange with a new concept—nomadic and global—which has

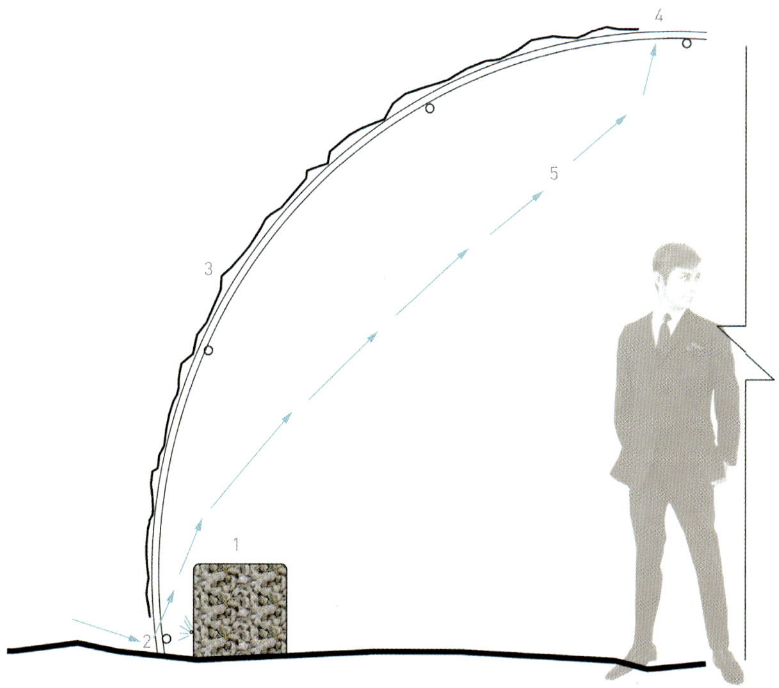

1 Stone bench
2 Opening
3 Felt roof
4 Upper opening
5 Air circulation

Conceptual cross section

Conceptual plan

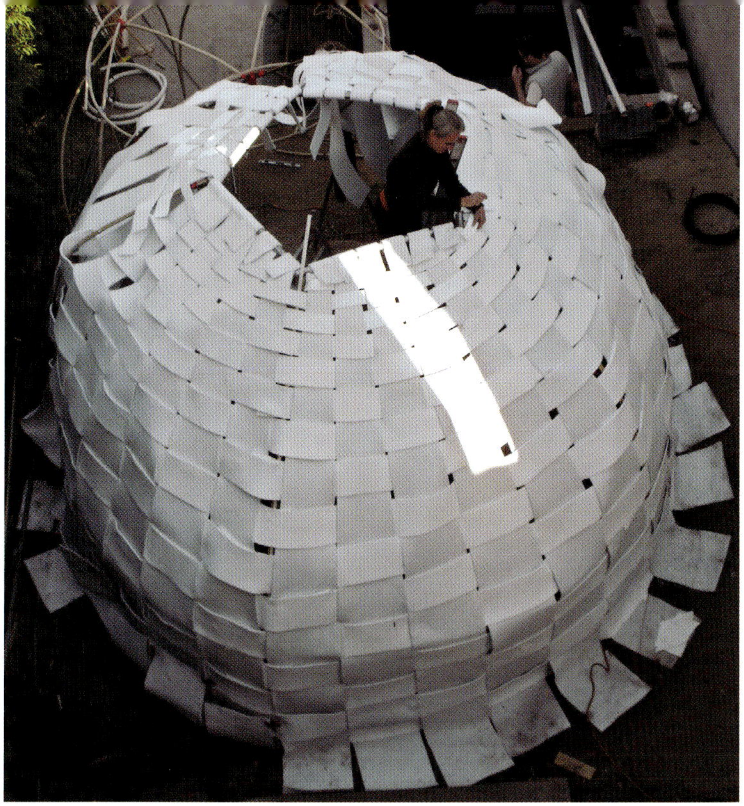

The roof, made with a rattan skeleton and felt bands, creates an appearance reminiscent of the blocks of ice that form an igloo.

brought about an igloo made of wool in a hot place.

The final product is a postmodern icon which explores the ancestral northern culture with new forms of construction. The simple observation of such a basic and simple architectural model like that of the ice house is a reminder of the often forgotten advantages of these vernacular buildings on a human scale: through an adaptability to the natural and climatic conditions these structures are set in, they get the most out of the environment.

I THINK THAT VERNACULAR ARCHITECTURE DESERVES OUR RESPECT, BUT WE CANNOT SIMPLY REPRODUCE IT.

Did the igloo inspire you when creating your installation?

AF: Yes, we were inspired by the traditional igloo from the north of Greenland. The idea was to create a Nordic igloo, but made of wool and in a Californian context.

JS: When they invited me to participate as an architect for Anja's conceptual igloo, the proposal interested me and the context of a postmodern city like Los Angeles could not have been more appropriate. Here we have a long history of manipulating and reinterpreting popular iconography to create new forms and environments. Anja's original concept was an interpretation of the Nordic myth, but I think that once we started, this idea turned into something much more complex and significant. The result was more an exploration of Euclidean geometry and phenomenological experience than a simple postmodern symbol.

What importance does vernacular architecture have in your work?

AF: It is very important that architecture expresses the essence of the vernacular to be able to visually communicate something about this culture.

JS: I live and work in Los Angeles, and I am very conscious of the local vernacular characteristics and of the role that they play in contemporary design, although it is much more subtle here than in other places. This city loves anything that is new and only now is it beginning to take note of the value of its rich history. Anja's alternative perspective, as well as the cultural diversity of the neighborhood where the project took place, influenced the design process and construction enormously.

What can we learn from vernacular architecture and how should we apply this knowledge to contemporary architecture?

AF: I think that we can learn a lot from these types of structures if what we are looking for is to create homes linked to nature, to society, and climatic change. We don't know what direction nature will take, but we can learn to build houses like in the north if the climate in the south changes drastically. Or, for example, if human beings become nomadic again, types of structures suitable for this lifestyle will be useful.

JS: I think that vernacular architecture deserves our respect, but we cannot simply reproduce it. Nowadays, contextualization is something which is difficult in our society, but I believe that it is possible to absorb vernacular concepts and apply them to design. We took the form of the traditional igloo as a starting point—the main dome and the adjoining hall—as a guide, the final product is a more evocative representation.

Why do you believe that the igloo has become an icon so closely linked to vernacular dwellings?

AF: I think that the igloo has a very strong social component; it represents the family unit, human warmth, and survival. It is a symbol of human kind in harmony with nature, where everyone has to collaborate to survive.

JS: It is comfortable and on a very human scale. Also, in Western culture, many people perceive the igloo as something exotic rather than historical. I remember when I was little watching the cartoons of Pepe the Penguin and his igloo. I always thought how much fun it would be to build one, but I lived in Florida, and there was no snow there.

IGLU-DORF

ARCHITECT Adrian Günter
LOCATION Davos-Klosters, Switzerland

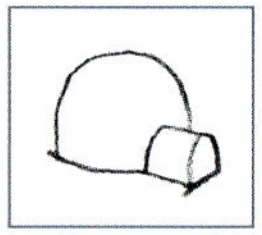

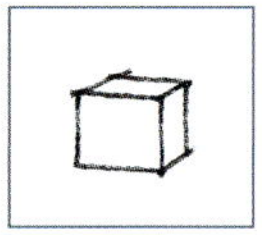

TYPE OF PROJECT Hotel
AREA 6,458 ft^2 (600 m^2)
HEIGHT 39 ft (12 m)
DURATION OF CONSTRUCTION 15 months
YEAR OF COMPLETION 2007
PHOTOS © Adrian Günter

Inspired by the dwellings of the Canadian Inuit, the architect Adrian Günter created idyllic villages in which the visitor can enjoy complete contact with nature. When the first snows cover the mountain peaks, five very original houses are established every year in frozen places in the Swiss Alps. After four months spring arrives and the snow village follows its natural course, melting over beautiful flowery meadows.

The outer walls are made of prefabricated molds of different sizes. These pieces are covered with artificial snow as it is more malleable and does not stick together. The interior of the buildings are white jewels created by imaginative ice sculptors. Günter uses recyclable molds

of different sizes (13, 26.25, or 33 feet [4, 8, or 10 m] in diameter) which create, once they are joined together, the semi-sphere shape of the vernacular snow houses. Nature's influencers—sun, wind, and cold—carve themselves onto the village in unison as the environmental context. The solitude, the temperature of this unique environment, and the sense of ad-

The wooden molds created for the construction of the village allow for an infinite variety of forms that are then covered with snow.

1 Entrance
2 Bar
3 Reception
4 Rooms
5 Bathroom
6 Office
7 Kitchen
8 Storage
9 Spa

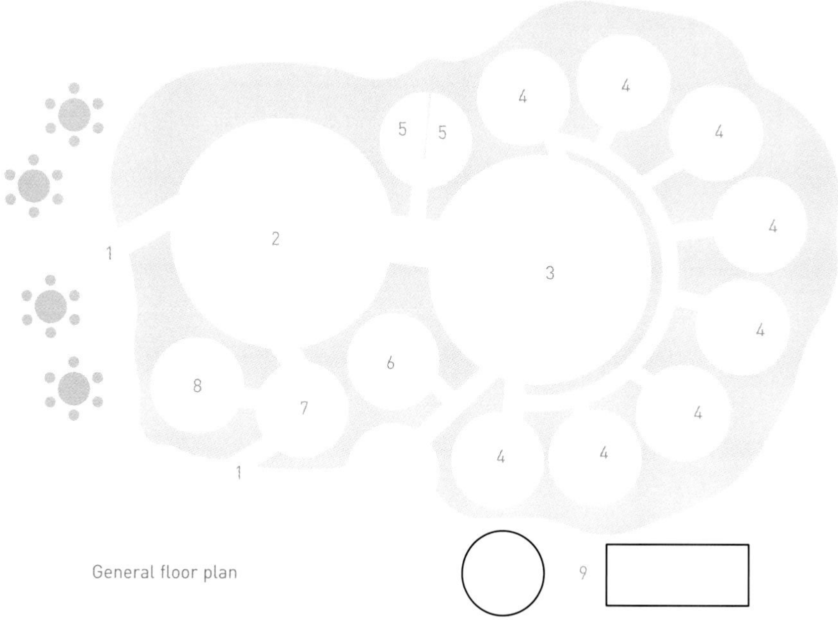

General floor plan

General elevation

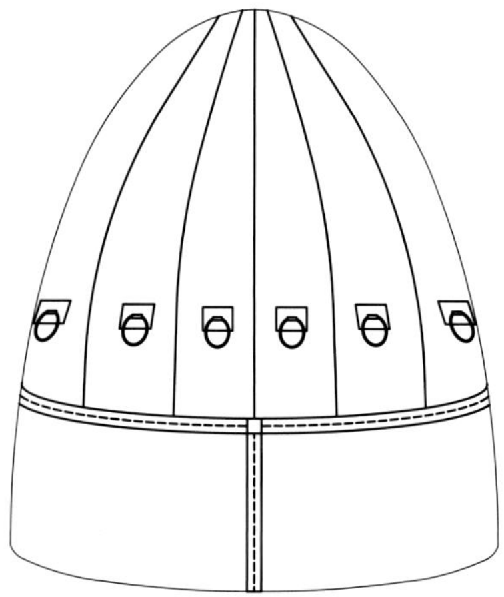

Vaulted wooden mold

venture mix together in the heart of anyone who spends the night in the new igloos. However, the client's comfort is of prime concern and the architect also planned rooms that are adapted to the needs of the most refined visitors, building an artificial waterfall that can maintain the warmest temperatures. This is a complete luxury in a simple environment in the midst of the magical Alps.

This structure provides an encounter with Inuit culture and art in a place of great charm. The exterior beauty of the snow village is the result of nature, the interior the result of man's intervention. Visiting this village is an extraordinary way to sleep in a place governed by the cycle of water—it will disappear after a brief period to turn into a new form of life.

The construction turns into, in this case, the raw material for the works of art that decorate the interior.

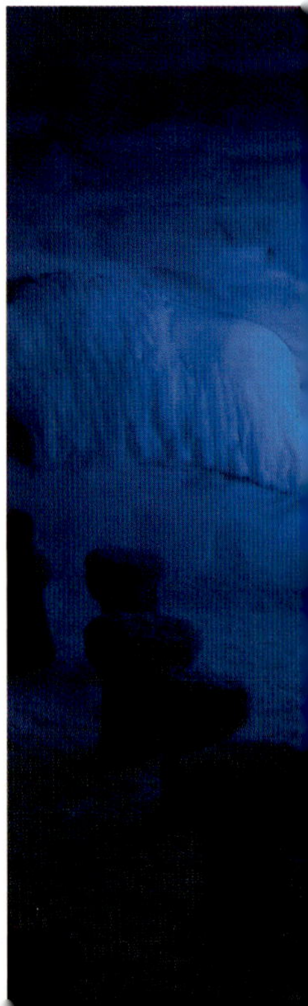

INTERVIEW WITYH **MARTIN VOGEL,**
director of architecture for Iglu-Dorf

> "THE IGLOO EVOKES IN EVERYONE A KIND OF ROMANTIC NOSTALGIA, IT GIVES US THE SENSATION OF WARMTH IN A FROZEN LANDSCAPE."

Is Iglu-Dorf inspired by the traditional igloo?
Not at the beginning. But when the hotel started to grow, Adrian became interested in Inuit culture and went to visit Canada's North Eastern Territory for a few months. Now we keep in touch with Inuit artists, who come to our igloos every year to contribute with their art. And even though our igloos are made with molds, we also offer our visitors the opportunity to build an igloo with blocks of ice.

What importance does vernacular architecture have in your work?
Our igloo village is very much connected to the nature that surrounds it: the sun the wind and the cold. They form part of the environment. In the interior we also adopt the curved shapes of the igloo, and in terms of the artwork, there is everything, although the Inuit influence is always present.

What can we learn from vernacular architecture?
Harmony with nature. Using natural materials to adapt to the environment. In some way, the exterior reflects the beauty of nature and the interior the beauty of the human being.

Why do you believe that the igloo has become an icon so closely linked to vernacular dwellings?
The igloo evokes in everyone a kind of romantic nostalgia; it gives us the sensation of warmth in a frozen environment and instills a sense of adventure in us.

PRESS PAVILLION

ARCHITECT a. ml und partner
LOCATION Oberstdorf, Germany

TYPE OF PROJECT Pavillion
AREA 1,184 ft^2 (110 m^2)
HEIGHT 16 ft (5 m)
DURATION OF CONSTRUCTION 9 months
YEAR OF COMPLETION 2005
PHOTOS ©Mila Hacke, Berlin

Commissioned by the organization committee of the Nordic Alpine Skiing World Championships in Germany (2005), the students of the Oberstdorf Institute of Design and Construction Technology (University of Biberach) developed this pavilion as a meeting point for the press, VIPs, and athletes. They achieved an irregular and surprising design thanks to the accumulation of 1,300 wooden pallets joined by tie rods and pull straps.

The building is made with local materials to obtain a sustainable architectural model. In a record time of ten weeks, the students of Construction and Design Architecture made this idea a reality, thanks to the enormous commitment of all those involved. The pavilion is anchored to the ground. At regular 8 ft (2.5 m) intervals, the pallets are pulled tight by the straps. This method ensures the stabilization of the irregular geometric form. The space

is 16 ft (5 m) high and 60 ft (18 m) long and has a great variety of possible uses. The experimental installation is similar to the igloo in the method of construction and in the raw material being found locally. The students made use of the collection of pallets in the same way that the Inuit nomads applied one block of ice to another—a method that is simple but effective. By observing the vernacular dwellings of the Inuit, the students considered

The arrangement and placement of each piece of wood is precisely calculated to produce a vaulted form.

Preliminary sketches

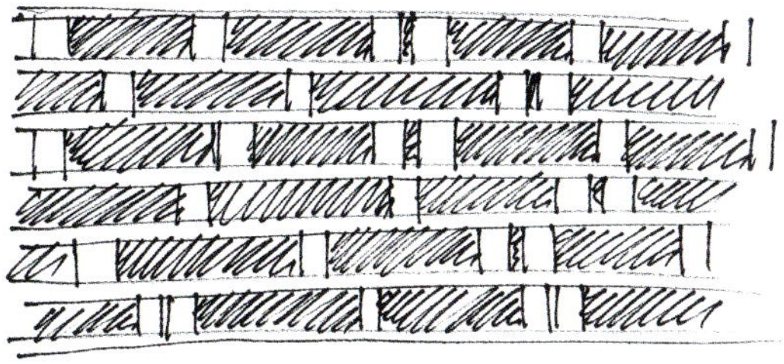

Interior elevation

The piece is a work of art which invites us to reflect on the tectonic character of any material and its visual possibilities.

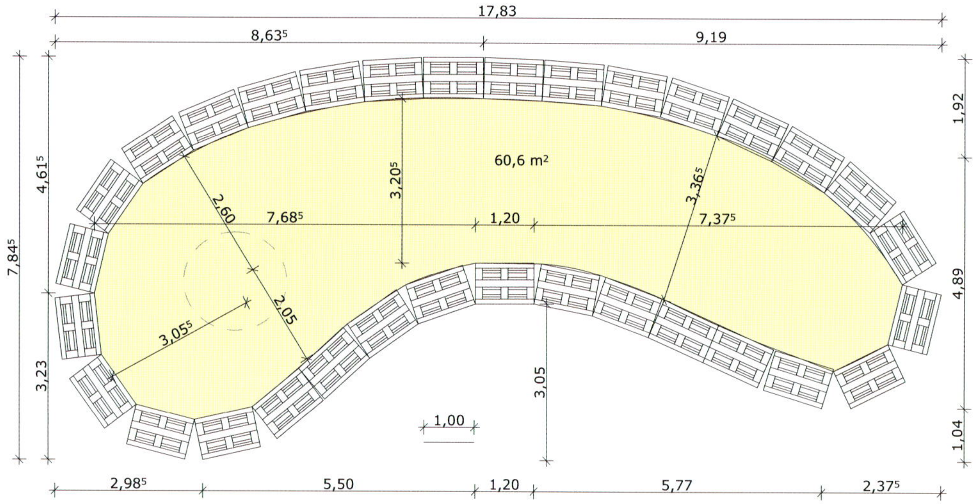

Plan

Side elevation

Front elevation

The warm light of the interior of the piece highlights the textures of the wooden pallets and shows the rhythm produced between the material and the gaps.

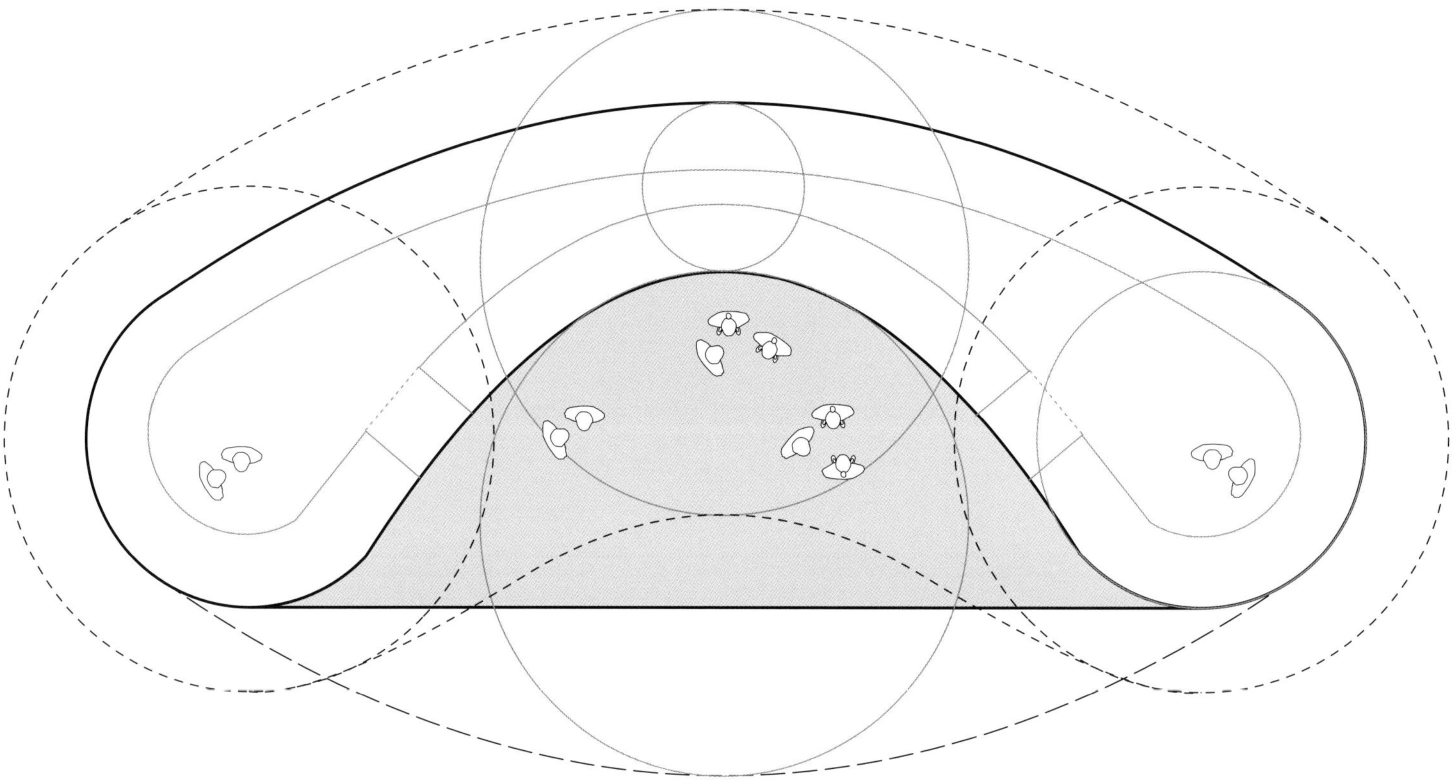

Geometric study of the floor plan

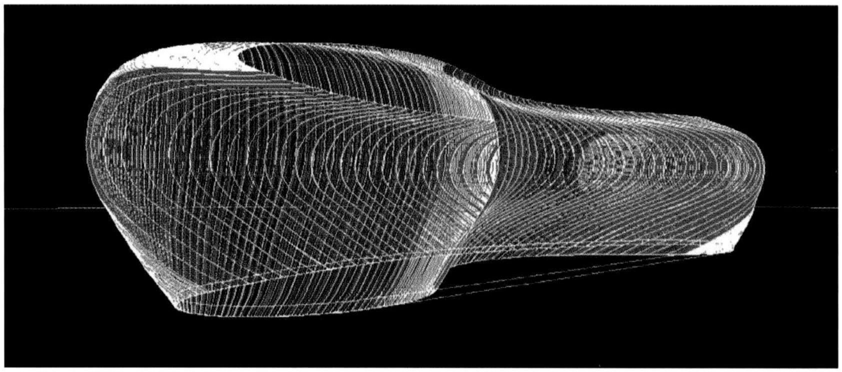

3D model

that a rounded morphology was the best way of recreating a welcome and enveloping atmosphere in the interior.

A research project of this magnitude can only come about if the various sponsors collaborate without being concerned with making a profit. The pallets, the ties, and the rods had to be returned to their owners in the fall of the same year. Just as if it were like the natural cycle of ice, this pavilion was born with a limited lifespan and subject to the laws of nature.

SAMI PARLIAMENT

ARCHITECT ALA Architects
LOCATION Kiruna, Sweden

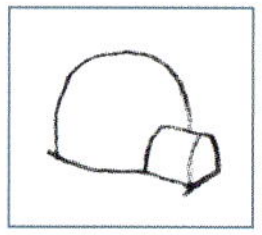

TYPE OF PROJECT Parliament Building
AREA 30,225 ft^2 (2,808 m^2)
HEIGHT 33 ft (10 m)
YEAR OF COMPLETION Project not yet built
ARCHITECTURAL RENDERING Marko Huttunen/Studico Oy

Parliament in the Swedish Sami region functions as a symbol for the community and as an institution for the rest of the world. In the extreme temperatures of Lapland, the architects of ALA Architects studio (Juho Grönholm, Antti Nousjoki, Janne Teräsvirta, and Samuli Woolston) designed this discussion forum inspired by the resources of the vernacular buildings of the Arctic. The building responds to the aesthetic and functional demands of its context. The mystical character of the building seeks power in the nature surrounding it. The border between the pretty town of Kiruna and the Sami Parliament fade away. The wooden, domed sculptures which stand out from the structure house the most important spaces of the building, some of them underground. The large upper holes are strategically directed to capture

the maximum available natural light, even in mid-winter. A large chimney, centrally situated between the library and the plenary hall, provides the heat needed during the cold nights in Lapland. The Parliament hall can be used as an all-purpose hall by the local people. North of the hall there is a three-floor office area separated by a central corridor with a glass wall. The feeling from inside is one of an open,

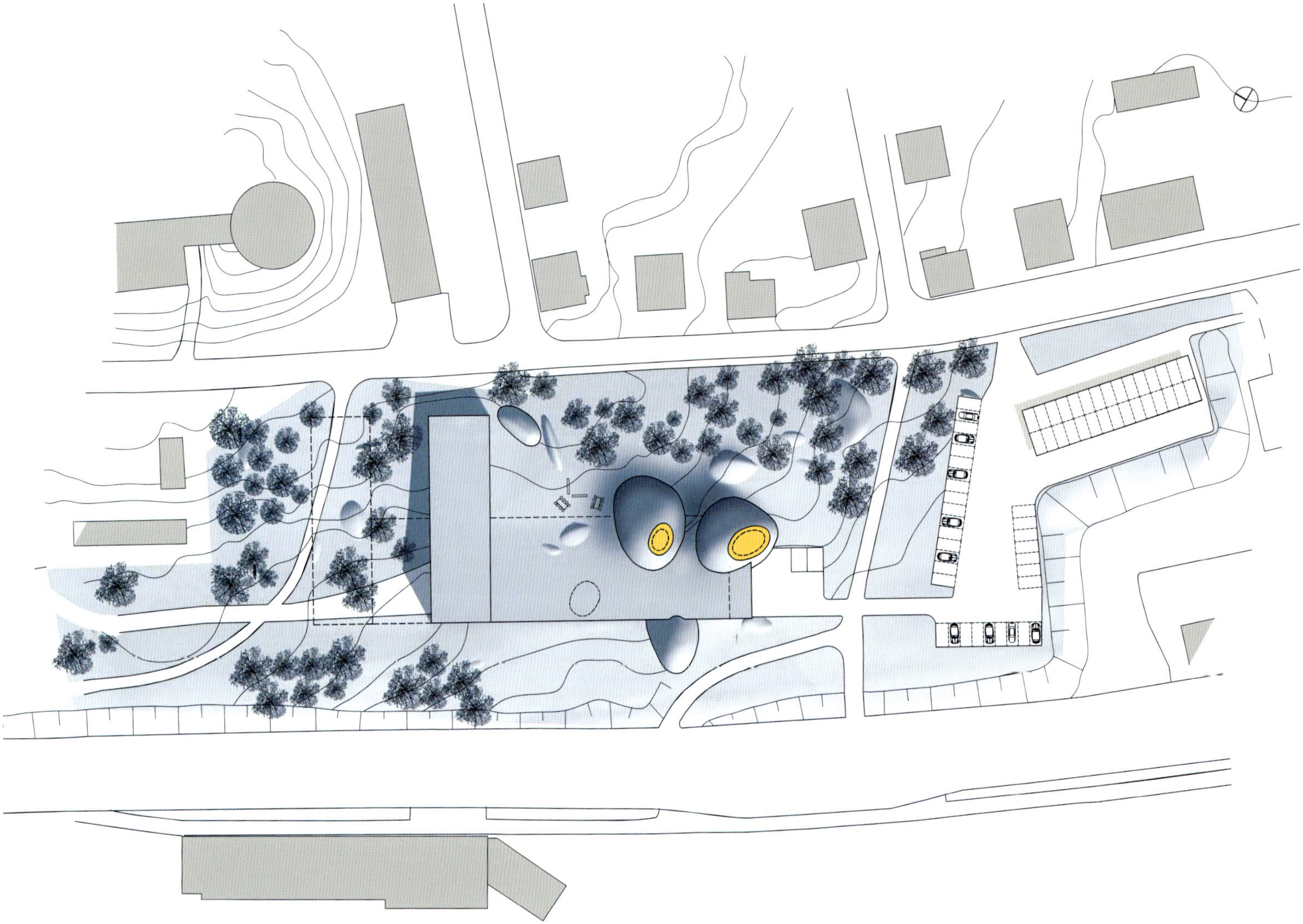

Site plan

light space. In the main entrance, the glass doors direct the visitor to a spacious lobby, situated right in the heart of the building. The facade is linked to the surrounding natural environment by simple joints of varying qualities of wood. The roof can be used as a terrace with an entrance to the office; it even has an open-air chimney and a traditional sauna.

The aim of this building is to communicate the voice of the people throughout their frozen surroundings. By looking at the igloo, the team from ALA Architects understood how the traditional way of building these structures provided solutions for their own project. The resulting project takes on the appearance of an Inuit settlement with small interconnected domes.

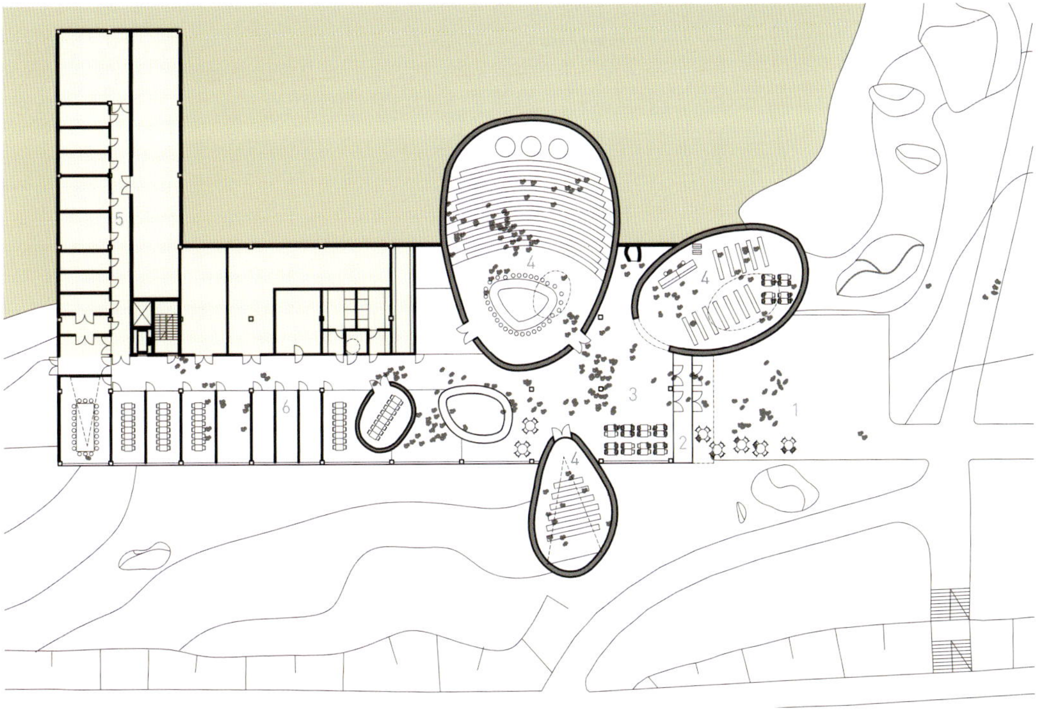

Ground floor

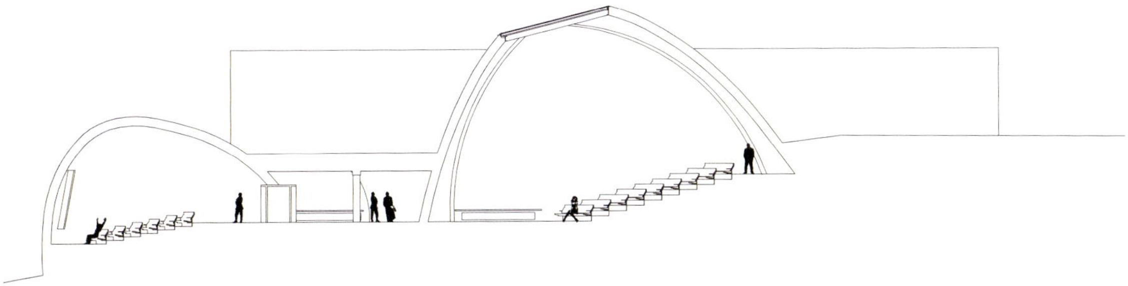

Transverse cross section

Scale model of the whole structure

The marble flooring of the interior is a visual reference to the frozen landscape of the exterior.

INTERVIEW WITH **JANNE TERÄSVIRTA**

> AN ARCHITECT SHOULD ALWAYS REMAIN CRITICAL AND KNOW HOW AND WHEN TO PROGRESS.

Did the igloo inspire you in the creation of this installation?
The starting point wasn't the igloo or any known type of vernacular architecture. Instead, we used the interpretation of the context and the program as a base. However, during the design process, the igloo came up, given its form and the thermal conditions of the project. In fact, we realized much later that the structural solutions of another type of Arctic structure could help us a lot: the Sami hut.

What importance does vernacular architecture have in your work?
We try to tackle each project in a different way. But it is true that when working in extreme conditions it is very useful to analyze traditional construction methods to better understand problems that arise and their possible solutions.

What can we learn from vernacular architecture and how can we apply this knowledge to contemporary architecture?
It is important to learn from it through observation. However, this doesn't mean that you should copy; an architect should always remain critical and know how and when to progress.

Why do you believe that the igloo has become an icon so closely linked to vernacular dwellings?
It is an easy structure to understand, unusual, romantic.... For most people it is something exotic and familiar at the same time.

IMAGE AND PHOTO CREDITS

Cover

Photo:
© B&C Alexander/Arcticphoto.com

Plan:
© Jestico+Whiles

Pages 6-23

Maps and illustrations:
Montse Montero

Photos:
© B&C Alexander/Arcticphoto.com;
pages 7, 9 (right), 10 (right), 11, 14, 15, 21 (right), 22, 23.

U.S. Library of Congress; pages 9 (left),13, 20 (left).

La Fédération des Coopératives du Nouveau Québec/J. Talirunili;
page 12 (right)

Pages 24-139

Photos credited in each project.

BIBLIOGRAPHY

Couchaux, Denis
Habitats nomades
Éditions Alternatives, 2004

Houston, James
Memorias del Ártico
Alba Editorial, 2000

Lefaivre, Liane; Tzonis, Alexander
Critical regionalism
Prestel, 2003

Nabokov, Peter; Easton, Robert
Native American architecture
Oxford University Press, 1989

Oliver, Paul
Dwellings: The vernacular house world wide
Phaidon, 2003

Steltzer, Ulli
Building an igloo
Henry Holt & Company, 1999

Upton, Dell
Common places: Readings in American vernacular architecture
University of Georgia Press, 1986

Yue, Charlotte; Yue, David
The igloo
Houghton Mifflin, 1988

WEBOGRAPHY

Arctic Anthropology Journal:
www.wisc.edu/wisconsinpress/journals/journals/aa.html

Canada's National Inuit Organization:
www.itk.ca

First Peoples of Canada:
www.civilization.ca

Houston North Virtual Gallery:
www.houston-north-gallery.ns.ca

Indian and Northern Affairs Canada:
www.ainc-inac.gc.ca

Inuit Circumpolar Council:
www.inuit.org

Inuit Circumpolar Council (Canada):
http://inuitcircumpolar.com

Nunavut, the Road to Our Land—Radio Canada International:
www.rcinet.ca/rci/es/dossiers/9429.shtml

Qikiqtani Inuit Association:
www.qia.ca

DIRECTORY

a. ml und partner
Moltkestraße 5 - Rückgebäude - 1. stock,
90429 Núremberg, Germany
T: +49 911 510 9031
F: +49 911 5109 032
buero@aml-partner.de
www.aml-partner.de

Adrian Günter
Iglu-Dorf
Rotzbergstraße 15
CH-6362 Stansstad, Switzerland
T: +41 (0) 41 612 2728
info@iglu-dorf.com
www.iglu-dorf.com

Åke Larsson
Icehotel
981 91 Jukkasjärvi, Sweden
T: +46 (0) 980 62 004
F: +46 (0) 70 669 96 42
art@icehotel.com
www.icehotel.com

ALA Architects
Tehtaankatu 40 B 17
00150 Helsinki, Finland
T: +358 9 4259 7330
F: +358 9 4259 7331
info@ala-a.com
www.ala-a.com

Anja Franke
Byskovvej 28
2730 Herlev, Denmark
T: +45 4492 1019
anjafranke@mail.dk
www.anjafranke.dk

Brière, Gilbert + associés
460 Ste-Catherine O, bureau 613
Montreal H3B 1A7, Quebec, Canadá
T: +1 514 875 1168
F: +1 514 875 2168
bga@brieregilbert.com
www.brieregilbert.com

Estudio FAM
Duque de Fernán Núñez 2, 5º 2ª
28012 Madrid, Spain
T/F: +34 91 369 0677
correo@estudiofam.com
www.estudiofam.com

Jestico+Whiles
1 Cobourg Street, London NW1 2HP,
United Kingdom
T: +44 020 7380 0382
F: +44 020 7380 0511
jw@jesticowhiles.com
www.jesticowhiles.com

John Southern
817 Silver Lake Blvd.
Los Ángeles, CA 90026, United States
T: +1 323 644 1415
F: +1 323 644 1814
info@urban-ops.net
www.urban-ops.net

Kengo Kuma & Associates
2-24-8 Minami Aoyama
Minato-ku, Tokio 107-0062, Japan
T: +81 03 3401 7721
F: +81 03 3401 7778
kinjo@kkaa.co.jp
www.kkaa.co.jp

Königsberger Vannucchi Arquitectura
Av. Eng. Luis Carlos Berrini 1461, 5th floor
São Paulo 04571-903, Brazil
T: +55 11 5505 7275
F: +55 11 5506 0952
kv@kvarch.com
www.kvarch.com

Marko Matulic Cvitanic
Pontificia Universidad Católica of Chile
Carmen Sylva 2381, dpto. 402
Santiago de Chile 3542000, Chile
T: +56 2 232 9415
marko.matulic@gmail.com

Oscar Niemeyer
Avenida Atlantica 3940,
Rio de Janeiro 22070-002, Brazil
T: +55 21 523 4890
F: +55 21 267 6388
www.niemeyer.org.br

Philippe SAMYN and PARTNERS
Chée/Stwg op Waterloo 1537
B-1180 Brussels, Belgium
T: +32 2374 9060
F: +32 2374 7550
sai@samynandpartners.be
www.samynandpartners.be

Serge Péloquin
Hôtel de Glace Quebec
143, Route Duchesnay, Pavillon La Régie
Ste-Catherine-de-la-Jacques-Cartier
G0A 3M0 Quebec, Canada
T: +1 418 875 4522
F: +1 418 875 2833
speloquin@icehotel-canada.com

Veech Media Architecture
Rudolfsplatz 6/2
A-1010 Viena, Austria
T: +43 1 315 5349
office@veech-vma.com
www.veech-vma.com